The Link between Environmental and Financial Performance

The Link between Company Environmental and Financial Performance, first published in 1998, is a detailed investigation into the effects of environmental performance – resource efficiency, regulatory compliance, new product and service opportunities – on corporate financial performance. This report makes essential reading for company management, investors and other stakeholders.

It demonstrates the quantitative links between environmental and financial performance for the UK's best and worst environmental performers across a range of business sectors. It shows that there is no financial penalty for being environmentally proactive, and confirms US findings that good environmental performance improves a company's financial performance.

The Link between Environmental and Financial Performance

David Edwards

Routledge
Taylor & Francis Group

First published in 1998
by Earthscan Publications Ltd

This edition first published in 2015 by Routledge
2 Park Square, Milton Park, Abingdon, Oxon, OX14 4RN
and by Routledge
711 Third Avenue, New York, NY 10017

Routledge is an imprint of the Taylor & Francis Group, an informa business

© 1998 David Edwards

Publisher's Note
The publisher has gone to great lengths to ensure the quality of this reprint but points out that some imperfections in the original copies may be apparent.

Disclaimer
The publisher has made every effort to trace copyright holders and welcomes correspondence from those they have been unable to contact.

ISBN 13: 978-1-138-02371-0 (hbk)
ISBN 13: 978-1-315-73886-4 (ebk)

THE LINK BETWEEN COMPANY ENVIRONMENTAL AND FINANCIAL PERFORMANCE

David Edwards

Earthscan Publications Ltd, London

First published in the UK in 1998 by
Earthscan Publications Ltd

A catalogue record for this book is available from the British Library

ISBN: 1 85383 549 8

Typesetting and page design by David Edwards
Printed and bound by Biddles Ltd, Guildford and Kings Lynn
Cover design by Andrew Corbett

For a full list of publications please contact:

Earthscan Publications Ltd
120 Pentonville Road
London, N1 9JN, UK
Tel: +44 (0)171 278 0433
Fax: +44 (0)171 278 1142
Email: earthinfo@earthscan.co.uk
http://www.earthscan.co.uk

Earthscan is an editorially independent subsidiary of Kogan Page Limited and publishes in association with WWF-UK and the International Institute for Environment and Development.

TABLE OF CONTENTS

LIST OF TABLES, FIGURES AND BOXES

TABLES

FIGURES

BOXES

ACKNOWLEDGMENTS

I am grateful to my supervisors at the Imperial College Centre for Environmental Technology, Dr Peter Pearson and Professor Richard Macrory, for their unstinting support, advice and enthusiasm during the initial research.

Many thanks also to Tim Robinson at Andersen Consulting, Emma Howard-Boyd, Charles Millar and Mike Tyrell at Jupiter Asset Management, my parents and Judy Sansom.

I am grateful to Jupiter Asset Management Limited for agreeing to the inclusion of its publication 'The Assessment Process for Green Investment' as an appendix to this book.

ACRONYMS AND ABBREVIATIONS

ACBE   Advisory Committee on Business and the Environment
ACCA   The Association of Chartered Certified Accountants
CEP   Council on Economic Priorities
DoE   Department of the Environment (Department of Environment, Transport and the Regions)
EFTA   European Free Trade Association
EIS   Environmental Information System
EPA   Environmental Protection Agency
EU   European Union
JERU   Jupiter Environmental Research Unit
JIGIT   Jupiter International Green Investment Trust
NGO   non-governmental organisation
NRA   National Rivers Authority
R&D   research and development
ROCE   return on capital employed
ROE   return on equity
TRI   Toxic Release Inventory
UNEP   United Nations Environment Programme
WBCSD   World Business Council on Sustainable Development

FOREWORD

It is a truism that money makes the world go around. From which it follows that to make the world go around in a different way it will be necessary to change the way that the money goes round. The busy people who make money go around in the City of London and the world's other financial centres are not by nature or training the most environmentally alert planetary citizens, nor are they easily moved by appeals to their aesthetic or moral sensibilities. Without significant changes in the daily choices they make, however, efforts to solve the accumulating problems of the environment will be seriously hampered. David Edward's study of the link between environmental and financial performance is a key element in bridging the knowledge chasm between the financial and environmental worlds. Far too much of the current discussion of environmental economics remains stranded in theory, isolated from the real worlds of financial and political decision making. Decision makers need analytical tools that are functional, robust and user-friendly. This painstakingly thorough demonstration that good environmental performance is positively correlated with good financial performance across a wide range of companies is an essential step in the creation of a set of analytical tools that will help to send the money round in a different, and more environmentally friendly, way.

Tom Burke CBE
Visiting Professor at Imperial College
London   June 1998

EXECUTIVE SUMMARY

Many companies have claimed that financial results can be significantly improved through resource efficiency initiatives, avoidance of fines and clean-up costs and new product and service opportunities. These companies also believe that an increasingly tough regulatory regime, greater public awareness, more accurate costing of environmental impacts and the growing environmental sophistication of key financial stakeholders such as insurers and banks, adds to the financial motivation to become more environmentally aware.

Empirical investigation in the US has suggested that there is a clear and positive correlation between environmental and financial performance. This study is the first to examine empirically whether UK companies can profit from environmentally proactive strategies. The study quantitatively links environmental and financial performance in order to draw conclusions as to the bottom line impact of green company policy.

The financial results of fifty 'green' companies, expertly assessed by Jupiter Asset Management as being environmentally the best in their sectors, were compared over a five year period with those of 'non-green' companies in the same sectors. The sectors investigated are defined using the All Share listing of the Financial Times. These sectors are: building merchants and materials; electrical and electronic equipment; engineering; paper, packaging and printing; healthcare; food retailers; general retailers and support services. The financial indicators used are return on capital employed and return on equity.

At the first stage of the analysis, the financial performance of each green company was compared to the average financial performance of a number of non-green companies of similar profile in the same sector between 1992 and 1996. At the second stage of analysis, each green company was compared to the best financial performer from the non-green sample in the first stage. By selecting the best financial performer from the non-green sample, stage two provides a more rigorous examination of any results obtained at stage one.

The results from this study suggest that:

- there is a positive link between the environmental and financial performance of companies in the sectors investigated;
- over two thirds of green companies perform better than their non-green counterparts in 1,200 direct comparisons of green and non-green companies at stage one of the analysis.
- in five sectors (building materials and merchants, electrical and electronic equipment, support services, healthcare and engineering) the green companies perform better than their non-green competitors in over 70 per cent of the comparisons at stage one of the analysis;
- the green companies perform as well as the non-green companies even at the more rigorous stage two of the analysis where the best financial performers are selected from the non-green sample for comparison.

In most cases it appears that companies which pursue environmental improvements, do financially better than their non-green competitors. At the very least this study shows there need be no financial penalty for corporate environmental excellence.

ABOUT THE AUTHOR

David Edwards read Biology with Management Studies at Imperial College, London as an undergraduate. He completed a Masters degree in Environmental Technology at the Imperial College Centre for Environmental Technology in 1996, specialising in Business and the Environment.

Whilst at Imperial College he led a canoe expedition to Cameroon in 1994 that carried out a study of the reptiles and amphibians of the riverside rainforest. In 1995 he took part in a climbing expedition to the Himachal Pradesh region of the Himalayas that made an environmental impact assessment of the Parbati valley. He is a keen skier, snowboarder and diver and is a Fellow of the Royal Geographical Society.

He currently works for Andersen Consulting in London.

CHAPTER 1
INTRODUCTION

It is unlikely that any company can be truly sustainable in its operations (Shrivastava and Hart 1992); however, the World Business Council on Sustainable Development (WBCSD), with 120 members in 35 countries representing more than 20 industrial sectors, has set itself a mission 'to provide business leadership as a catalyst for change toward sustainable development, and to promote eco-efficiency in business' (Schmidheimy and Zorraquin 1996). Thus has the need for serious progress in standards of environmental performance by industry been publicly acknowledged by industry itself.

The motivation for companies to take the path towards sustainability may be encouraged by a variety of factors. Some are negative and reactive, such as the fear of non-compliance or the wish to avoid bad publicity; some are positive and proactive, such as new market opportunities and resource cost savings. This research aims to explore these motivators and examine quantitatively and qualitatively the effect of environmental performance, good and bad, on the financial bottom line of a company.

Background

In recent years a number of influential voices in the environmental arena have proposed the apparently paradoxical notion that the goals of business and environment might be reconcilable. These protagonists have insisted that companies can profit from enhanced environmental performance in ways such as more efficient waste management, pollution prevention, premiums on green products and improved public image (Porter 1991, Schmidheimy and Zorraquin 1995).

The idea that systematic improvements in environmental performance will lead to improvements in the financial bottom line is appealing to industrialists and green activists alike. However, company leaders who were initially positive about the possible revenue accruing from sound environmental practice have begun to question the environmental 'free lunch' (Cairncross 1994) as they experience diminishing returns on environmental projects and as 'first mover' advantages are eroded due to more and more firms adopting environmental programmes.

Initial enthusiasm about cost savings and competitive advantage has recently given way to a more cautious approach. It has become clear that the slogan adopted by Dow Chemicals, 'Waste Reduction Always Pays', simply is not true for many businesses. Such optimism may lead to unrealistic expectations and a breakdown in the dialogue between environmentalists and business leaders. Professor Rob Gray (1994) at the Centre for Social and Environmental Accounting Research in Dundee has commented:

Given that we have no way of knowing whether or not the planetary ecology is truly in crisis, and that it is impossible for us to ascertain whether our present ways of doing business can be made compatible with environmental sensitivity, we as a business community have some hard thinking to do. And the sooner we abandon the virtually empty rhetoric of win – win situations the better for business and the environment.

[Gray 1994]

The reality of the situation probably lies between the extremes. It is unlikely that executives at Dow Chemicals truly believed that all pollution prevention capital expenditure yields a positive return. Catchy slogans can bring public relations benefits and provide impetus for efforts towards efficiency by employees. It is also unlikely that Professor Gray totally refutes the idea of win – win situations. A report in the US which reviewed more than 100 studies into the effect of environmental regulations on economic competitiveness, concluded that there was no conclusive evidence to support either position.

Studies gauging the effects of environmental regulation on net exports, overall trade flows, and plant-location decisions have produced estimates that are small or statistically insignificant.

[Stavins, Jaffe, Peterson and Portney 1994]

The Framework for Change

The approach of industry to environmental quality issues in the 1970s was characterised by reactive and resistant attitudes in the industrial world. There was, on the whole, little awareness of the potential savings that could be made from environmental initiatives and unwillingness to cooperate with even the most enlightened policy-making. The 1980s saw a more positive approach from many companies and a growing realisation that innovative solutions in areas such as waste management, pollution, and environmental management systems could aid resource efficiency and reap large financial rewards for forward thinking companies. At Glaxo's site in Cumbria, the factory's solvent recovery plant recycles materials which might otherwise cause air and water pollution and in the process cut the company's solvent bill by £20 million a year in 1986. On a smaller scale, cider-makers H.P. Bulmer used biotechnology to devise an effluent treatment plant able to clean up hot acidic wastes from their pectin plant. The total capital cost for the plant was £24,000, while the savings in its first year were estimated to have been £30,000 (Elkington and Burke 1987).

Environmental improvement has often been the by-product of the pursuit of other goals. In the late 1970s the objectives were often reduced energy use in reaction to the oil price shocks, in the 1980s many industries pursued better productivity as part of that decade's drive for leaner companies, but in many cases, and in some unexpectedly, these profitable investments led to greener production. There are many such examples of environmental investments leading to impressive savings from a wide variety of sectors. However, many corporations are questioning how long the momentum of such initiatives can be sustained.

As diminishing returns on environmental investment have set in, the new generation of environmental managers have found it difficult to replicate the impressive successes of the 1980s and are increasingly nervous of stakeholder reaction to expensive environmental investments. Shareholders and the financial community are concerned that environmental spending is spiralling out of control to the detriment of other operational and capital investment considerations. Non-governmental organisation (NGO) concern focuses on the loss of momentum of the greening process and a reduced prominence of environmental issues on the company agenda (Walley and Whitehead 1994).

The road to a coherent and successful environmental strategy is a difficult one for many firms. Companies have been extremely nervous about the increasing transparency forced upon them by environmental legislation, such as Integrated Pollution Control authorisation requirements and statutory environmental impact assessments. They believe, often rightly so, that much of the information they are being asked to share with the world, especially regarding products and processes, confers competitive advantage to the company and that commercial security may be compromised by such 'blood-letting'.

The financial markets may look on with distrust, and in some cases actually penalise, companies that are setting aside significant funding for environmental projects (Schmidheimy and Zorraquin 1995). Firms may also be increasing their vulnerability to adverse publicity. It is much easier to attack a firm like the Body Shop for a single transgression from its stated environmental policy because the company has a high media profile built on the back of its excellence. The share price of the Body Shop fell significantly after accusations of discrepancies between its animal testing policy and the actual activities of the company. In the wake of the controversy surrounding the disposal of the Brent Spar oil platform the Advisory Committee on Business and Environment commented:

Balanced reporting of environmentally sensitive decisions is to be welcomed since it helps to inform responsible public discussion. On the other hand, sensational reporting is counter-productive since, in the glare of publicity, constructive debate on potentially contentious matters becomes very difficult. Through over-simplifying issues and focusing on drama and conflict, such media stories tend to polarise views. In such an atmosphere it is much easier to appeal to the value systems of 'interested parties' than it is to argue detailed points of science, law or economics. In addition, sensational media stories tend to highlight situations as 'win – lose'. It is close to impossible to create a 'win – win' situation in the glare of publicity.
[Seventh Progress Report to, and Response from, the President of the Board of Trade and the Secretary of State for the Environment March 1997]

Assessing the Benefits of Green Strategy

Finance directors and accountants who attempt to quantify a company's environmental efforts face an ill-defined and complex task. Environmental financial reporting and accounting have evolved slowly due to a lack of understanding and a reluctance by accountants to get involved in issues which they have not traditionally considered of relevance to the profession. These attitudes are rapidly changing. Daniel Blake Rubenstein (a chartered accountant and Principal in the Office of the Auditor General in Canada) comments:

For the first time in accounting's sleepy history, there is a growing recognition among accountants and non-accountants alike that accounting, that a value-free, balanced system of double entries, may be sending dangerously incomplete signals to business, to consumers, to regulators, and to bankers. The imperative to reconsider 5000 years of accounting conventions is not a passing fad.
[Rubenstein 1994]

Environmental accounting is one way in which positive and negative changes to the profit and loss account are ascribed to changes in the environmental performance of the firm. A change to a less toxic raw material used in a process is likely to incur more or less raw material expenditure. This will affect financial performance and it is vital that management is able to calculate the impact on the bottom line. Within the context of this report it is important to note that the value of environmental accounting lies not only in assigning financial values to the impacts of companies, processes or products, but also as an internal management tool for spotting environmental projects and initiatives with realistic rates of return.

Since 1990, stakeholders have pushed for more companies to accurately report their environmental liabilities and exposure to increasingly tough environmental legislation. When the Association of Chartered Certified Accountants launched its Environmental Reporting Award scheme in 1991 only seven companies entered, mainly the few already issuing environmental reports in Britain. For the 1997 award, 64 companies have been nominated.

There are essentially three strands to environmental accounting: national income accounting, finance accounting and managerial accounting. National income accounting, or natural resource accounting, occurs when physical or monetary units are used to refer to the consumption of a nation's environmental resources. Finance accounting reports environmental liabilities and financially material environmental costs to an external audience including investors and lenders. Managerial accounting is the process of identifying, collecting and analysing environmental information principally for internal purposes (US EPA 1995). It is developments in financial and managerial environmental accounting that will have the greatest impact on a company's presentation of the financial consequences of its environmental actions.

Accurate and pertinent business and environmental decisions are far more likely to be made by managers when they act upon accurate and pertinent information. Companies that employ managerial environmental accounting are far more likely to be able to take advantage of opportunities to produce in a cost-effective way.

Box 1.1: Benefits of Environmental Managerial Accounting

The *US EPA Primer on Environmental Accounting* (1995) concentrates on managerial accounting and lists a number of benefits that such a tool may have, including the control and reduction of environmental costs. It suggests that:

i) Many environmental costs can be significantly reduced or eliminated as a result of business decisions ranging from operational and housekeeping changes, to investment in 'greener' process technology, to redesign of process/products.

ii) Environmental costs (and thus, potential cost savings) may be obscured in overhead accounts or otherwise overlooked.

iii) Many companies have discovered that environmental costs can be offset by, for example, generating revenues through sale of waste by-products or transferable pollution allowances, or licensing of clean technologies.

iv) Better management of environmental costs can result in improved environmental performance and significant benefits to human health as well as to business success.

v) Understanding the environmental costs and performance of processes and products can promote more accurate costing and pricing of products and can aid companies in the design of more environmentally preferable processes, products and services for the future.

vi) Competitive advantage with customers can result from processes, products and services that can be demonstrated to be environmentally preferred.

vii) Accounting for environmental costs and performance can support a company's development of an overall environmental management system.

Source: *US EPA Primer on Environmental Accounting* 1995

Another enthusiastic advocate of environmental managerial accounting is Richard Wells, Director of Corporate Environmental Consulting, Abt Associates Inc. He believes that companies must have management systems capable of taking advantage of flexible government regulations. These systems must link environmental opportunities to financial data in order for the company to be able to scan them against corporate return on investment objectives.

> *Most US companies don't have adequate tools to scan their operations for environmental opportunities or to prioritise or evaluate them in terms of contribution to shareholder value. Companies like Polaroid, Du Pont and J.M. Huber, however, are demonstrating that rigorous analysis can uncover win – win opportunities. Such analysis looks at the full revenue- and cost- side contributions of environmental initiatives to shareholder value.*
>
> [Wells 1994]

Ciba Geigy takes the idea of information gathering to impressive degrees with its Environmental Information System (EIS). Daily information about the emissions and raw material use from all of the company's production processes is downloaded into a central database and reformatted so that environmental performance can be audited and checked against benchmarks set by the environmental management system.

Ciba Geigy is able to assign both financial and environmental costs to specific products and processes, and in so doing is automatically alerted to both positive and negative outcomes of its day-to-day operations. For example, the system highlights potential breaches of compliance and at the same time draws attention to possibilities for raw material reduction, reuse or substitution.

There is a growing recognition that there is a need to internalise environmental costs where possible in a systematic way so that businesses can count the true cost of their products and adjust price and income values accordingly (CBI 1994). Thorn EMI, winner of the 1995 ACCA Environmental Reporting Award, and British Telecom are examples of companies attempting environmental accounting, but there is general recognition that there will have to be regulatory motivation for businesses to get seriously interested in environmental accounting. The use of management accounting techniques (such as capital budgeting and cost centre allocation) as applied to green projects allows managers to more accurately ascertain the value of such investment and make more informed choices for resource allocation.

Integration of the Environmental Function

As environmental management has matured into a sophisticated and well understood management function, it has been increasingly integrated into all aspects of a company's operations and into the day-to-day working practices of employees. Environmental management has obvious links with health and safety management and total quality management, but increasingly a company's finance directors, lawyers, purchasers, personnel departments and strategists have found the 'environment' manifest in their day-to-day tasks. Environmental management has moved towards a generalist rather than a technical specialist function (Elkington 1996).

Product managers have found they can sell products which have a better environmental performance than competitors' products, at a premium. In Germany Hoover's sales rose significantly in the first year after receiving an eco-label, under the EU scheme, for sales rose significantly in the first year after receiving an eco-label, under the EU scheme, for their washing machine. Castrol developed a biodegradable engine oil for outboard engines on motorboats after concern about oil pollution in the Swiss lakes. This product quickly became the market leader as not only did the reformulated oil have superior environmental performance, it also had better technical performance in terms of stability, cleanliness and anti-corrosion properties. There have, however, been setbacks in the rise of green products, notably recycled paper and green detergents which have often performed badly when compared to standard products. There have often been conflicting analyses as to the environmental impacts of these products, sending confusing signals to potential green consumers. Managing consumer perception and expectation successfully is difficult as these factors are often irrational and unpredictable but a carefully targeted marketing strategy will reduce the chances of failure.

Marketing departments have been slow to capitalise on the benefits of good environmental practice, although the success of high-profile campaigns like that of the Co-operative bank, whose account openings have risen dramatically on the strength of its advertised promises not to invest in unnecessarily polluting companies, have shown that the green market is often a significant one. Green marketing is increasing in sophistication and innovation and new avenues like the deregulated electricity market are being explored by firms like Eastern Electricity who announced a green 'Eco-power' tariff designed for consumers prepared to pay an extra 5 per cent on their electricity bill for research and investment into renewable power supply.

British companies have been accused of being slow in comparison to Germany and the US with regard to marketing green technology. There are many new business opportunities in water treatment, in pollution monitoring and abatement technology, recycling systems and growing markets in consultancy. The reluctance of British companies to get involved may be due to the slow pace of environmental legislation in the home market rather than a lack of innovative thinking by the companies themselves, although the Department of the Environment (DoE) noted in a discussion paper (1997) that it may be difficult to predict how business will respond to new policy measures. They may stimulate innovation, or provide impetus for an investment already being considered by a firm, it might also lead to investment being made in avoidance of intended policy direction. This paper notes that 'there is plenty of evidence, for example on take up of energy efficiency and waste minimisation measures, to demonstrate that firms do not introduce all cost effective measures or investment proposals justified by economic analysis and that an external push can overcome internal barriers to implementation'.

The world market for environmental goods and services is predicted to be £320 billion by the year 2000 and as Sir Terence Beckett noted in 1985:

> *We cannot afford to be coy about selling our ideas to a world market, the developed world is environmentally highly-charged at the moment and if we don't take the opportunities which present themselves, our rivals surely will.*

Companies with an environmental management system may find that their external financing is positively affected. Cost of capital may be lowered, insurance premiums reduced and share price improved (Piesse 1992) by the positive evaluation of a firm's environmental performance. These three aspects of a firm's financial structure may also be negatively affected by poor or non-existent environmental policy. As part of total environmental management systems, the most forward-looking companies are starting to look at their investment strategy, to the extent that green funds have been contacted by multinational companies for advice on socially and environmentally responsible investment opportunities.

At the United Nations Environment Programme (UNEP) meeting on 'Banks and the Environment' in 1994, Deutsche Bank outlined a system for checking the environmental risk rating of companies, specifically linking this concept to credit worthiness on the basis of the environmental risk associated with the company. Deutsche Bank were interested not only in 'hard' evidence and direct risk such as contaminated land liability issues but also 'soft', indirect risks inherent in the environmental management of a company and how future legislation might affect the company's environmental performance. Deutsche Bank stated at the UNEP meeting that:

Banks must be able to realistically assess what ecological influences and trends their corporate customers will be faced with, and what effect this will have on the customer's ability to do business successfully and service loans on time.

[UNEP 1994]

Deutsche Bank's risk scoring sheet for the environmental assessment of companies is thorough and is summarised to give an indication of the sort of information that managers might be increasingly expected to have when applying to lending facilities.

Box 1.2: Deutsche Bank's Environmental Risk Scoring Sheet

Three categories are scored: **Market position, Management and Future Perspective.**

i) Market position
a. Business sector
- Is the market changing through new regulation, the use of economic incentives or altered consumer behaviour?
- Does the company conduct appropriate planning, and will it be able to react to these new developments?

b. Product and service range
- Does the product range take into account important success factors such as environmental requirements, and does the marketing concept take these into consideration?
- Is the company engaged in systematic R&D work, also with a view to environmental protection?
- Are there ecological risks involved in procurement, production, products or sales?
- Are there risks from environmental liability legislation and are these sufficiently insured?

c. Target group
- Does the company offer problem solution concepts in line with customer needs, e.g. does the company provide support in recycling and waste disposal, assuming this is an important success factor?

ii) Management
- Does the management set regular targets?
- Are the planning systems transparent and sufficiently connected?
- Are the company's organisation and deputisation regulations in line with its business requirements?

iii) Future perspective
- Are the company's investment decisions in line with expected market developments?
- Do the company's products and services satisfy and possibly enhance the needs of its target group, and is the company working on improving and expanding its performance?

Source: *Deutsche Bank Environment Risk Scoring Sheet* 1994

Conclusions

Table 1.1 provides a summary of two very different attitudes to corporate environmental responsibility. The table highlights extreme positions and most corporations will fall somewhere in the middle of the two. The table illustrates both the breadth of issues that environmental management must address and also how easy it is for either green activists, or industry polluters, to simplify this important and complex debate.

Table 1.1: The Debate for Business

PROACTIVE DRIVERS	REACTIVE RESISTORS
Good environmental management leads to improved overall management	Environmental management distracts and leads to a loss of focus on more important management objectives
Improved waste management produces better resource efficiency	Savings from improved waste management are too small and hard-won
Energy efficiency produces significant cost savings	Energy efficiency savings are relatively insignificant and too difficult to measure
Increasing environmental legislation requires increasing investment in pollution reduction technology and clean-up operations	Low level of enforcement and benefits from smaller unit cost of production relative to competitors make non-compliance worthwhile
Preferential environmental risk ratings make credit easier to secure	Not all lenders are environmentally aware or concerned
Green companies will attract the best and the brightest recruits	Recruits are generally unaware of a company's environmental record. Other factors (salary, length of contract) are more important
Better media coverage, the Internet and enhanced global communications ensure that polluters will be publicly condemned	Bad media coverage and consumer boycotts are short-lived and worth the risk
Good environmental performance leads to better employee morale	Green initiatives decrease employee morale if they do not produce results
Transparency with regard to environmental performance leads to enhanced stakeholder relations and rewards for good performance	Transparency with regard to environmental performance is a commercial liability and may lead to reductions in competitive advantage
The financial markets reward green companies through higher share price and increased investment	There is significant City prejudice and distrust of green companies
A green image leads to positive media attention and increased public respect	A good environmental image sets the company up for criticism

A clearly demonstrated link between environmental and financial performance has proved elusive. Some studies have been carried out in the US where government regulation and Securities Exchange listings requirements have yielded systematic and comparable environmental data in recent years. This research is examined in Chapter 2.

In the UK, environmental data have not been of sufficient quality or quantity to accurately identify 'clean' and 'dirty' companies. Consensus has been reached by industry, the financial markets and the green movement on the point that corporate environmental disclosure is best achieved through an annual environmental report. However only 20 per cent of companies undertake to produce such a document (Company Reporting 1994); they differ in style, form and content and contain little, if any, quantitative data with which to attempt comparison of the environmental performance of companies, even within industry sectors.

Aim and Structure of the Report

This report examines the hypothesis that companies with good environmental performance perform financially better than companies with bad or indifferent environmental performance. The study will provide evidence as to whether or not there is a penalty for companies with a proactive environmental strategy. It will do this with the use of environmental research from one of only two green investment funds in the UK with an in-house research facility. This environmental research will be linked to financial results for companies in a variety of industries. Chapter 2 will examine the historical context of this debate and assess the evidence for a link between environmental and financial performance. The methodology employed will be outlined in Chapter 3 and an analysis of the results provided in Chapter 4. Chapter 5 discusses the implications of the results in the context of the individual company, the financial markets and the national policy agenda.

CHAPTER 2
REVIEW

Overview

This chapter is a review of some of the relevant literature and important issues arising from it. It places this report in the context of similar work in the US and the UK and discusses conclusions previous authors have made with regard to the link between the environmental and financial performance of a company.

The Debate

As has been noted in the introduction, environmental excellence and industrial development have often been presented as goals that may be achieved in tandem. This view has been eagerly accepted by many industry leaders. According to David Roderick of United States Steel:

> *We face a modern challenge to develop a cooperative effort for protecting the world's environment while achieving economic growth. We reject outright the false notion that environmental improvement and industrial development are mutually exclusive.*

Many writers have added a note of caution to this win – win evangelism, notably Walley and Whitehead (1994) who argue that 'low hanging fruit' such as the $500 million of resources saved by the company, 3M, since 1975, and the £2 million cost savings made by 11 companies in the Aire and Calder waste reduction scheme in the UK, has already been picked by the majority of companies. Revenue saving or enhancing opportunities are becoming scarcer, will have smaller returns and require more innovation and creativity to realise. 'Win – win opportunities become insignificant in the face of the enormous environmental expenditures that will never generate a positive financial return' (Walley and Whitehead 1994).

An era of 'resistant adaptation' in the 1970s and early 1980s, during which even compliance was considered an admirable target (Kleiner 1991), was characterised by an unwillingness by companies to internalise environmental issues. This gave way to a second era in the late 1980s in which companies 'embraced environmental issues without innovating' (Fischer and Schot 1994) and environmental programmes frequently produced startling improvements in efficiency and productivity. It was during this second era that win – win rhetoric came into its own and the 'Pollution Prevention Pays' motto was adopted by many companies.

The 1990s have seen companies attempting to take on board conceptually challenging ideas like sustainable development. They have found 'environment' pervading all aspects of their operations rather than being confined to pollution and waste management. This attitude change is reflected in the increasing difficulty which companies have in defining environmental expenditure and the decision by many companies to include environmental reporting within the main annual report rather than have a separate document.

An Economist's View

When assessing whether enhanced environmental performance will lead to increased profits, a firm must consider the effects of that change on the revenues and costs of the firm. In order to raise profits, the firm must raise revenues relative to costs. From economic theory, the overall maximisation of profits will occur when activities are expanded to that output at which the marginal revenue from an extra unit equals its marginal cost. Here, a 'unit' could be an increase in the environmental attributes or performance of a product, process or company. So to summarise, each environmental attribute should be developed or expanded up to the point where the marginal revenue from an additional 'unit' of the environmental attribute equals the marginal cost of the unit. If environmental attributes are improved beyond this point then the marginal costs become larger than the marginal revenues and the firm's profits are reduced. Thus, for resource efficiency investments such as reduced energy use or reduced waste from a process, there is a level at which reducing the energy use or waste production will become unprofitable. For pollution reduction the costs can increase exponentially as the company attempts to eliminate the last unit of pollution. The calculation of marginal costs and revenues is therefore important for a company, in making decisions to improve environmental performance.

Revenues

The calculation of marginal revenues involves some measure of the willingness of the customer to pay for the extra environmental attributes. This is problematic since the variation of the willingness to pay might be wide within the target market, and there is difficulty in assigning quantitative values to environmental attributes. Increased environmental performance of a product may increase revenue for the company by persuading existing customers to buy larger quantities, by attracting customers from competitors, by persuading new consumers to try the product, or by persuading customers to pay higher prices.

Costs

The costs associated with providing enhanced environmental attributes to a product, process or company, must be balanced against any associated revenue increases to give an indication of the effect on profitability. Costs may rise due to technology changes, implementation of management systems or increased number of employees. Costs may fall due to increases in resource efficiency or less employee time lost through illness from a polluting process. The management of the firm will invest in additional environmental attributes when the rate of increase in the costs is less than the rate of increase in the revenues.

There are of course a number of indirect and external factors that must be taken into consideration when evaluating these costs and revenues. These include the reaction of other firms and the effect of improving environmental performance on the regulatory climate. Sustained compliance by companies may encourage regulators to take the view that higher standards could be achieved causing a tightening of regulation. Alternatively the regulator could lower standards if it is thought that companies are meeting standards better through self motivation (Pearson and Fouquet 1996).

An important fact to highlight from this aspect of the interaction between environmental and financial performance, is that the evaluation of potential revenues is problematic because the measurement of the public willingness to pay is often inaccurate. Marginal revenue curves will reflect the public's willingness to pay and are likely to vary for different environmental attributes and across different populations and income levels. So there may be greater willingness to pay for reductions in locally damaging emissions of air, and water pollutants, than for reductions in trans nationally or globally damaging pollutants. (Pearson and Fouquet 1996). This can be revealed through detailed empirical analysis, although it is difficult in practice. Mining companies have attempted to quantify willingness to pay in Australia in cost-benefit analysis of proposed projects in national parks and Aboriginal burial grounds, and it was used controversially to assess clean-up costs in the *Exxon Valdez* oil spill case.

Linking Pollution Prevention to Profitability

The idea that an effective environmental management programme might impact positively on the bottom line is one that is beginning to be taken more seriously by the business world. The concept has, however, attracted limited academic research even in the US, where the necessary comparable environmental information is available.

Studies that have been carried out have often been contradictory. Erfle and Fratantuono (1992), used as base data, the Council on Economic Priorities (CEP) environmental indices which are based on regulatory compliance and existence, or lack of environmental programmes such as recycling or waste reduction. Their conclusion was that environmental performance was significantly positively correlated with return on assets, return on equity and return on investment.

Mahaptra in 1984 had concluded exactly the opposite and indeed that 'pollution control expenditures are a drain on resources which could have been invested profitably and do not reward the companies for socially responsible behaviour'. The contradictions may, in many cases, have much to owe to small sample size and lack of objective criteria and data for evaluating environmental performance (Cohen, Fenn and Naimon 1995).

In April 1995 Mark Cohen at Vanderbilt University, Tennessee and Scott Fenn and Jonathan Naimon at the Investor Responsibility Research Center in Washington completed perhaps the most comprehensive assessment to date of the impact of corporate environmentalism on the financial bottom line. In their paper, *Environmental and Financial Performance: Are They Related?*, they used data that had not previously been available, even in the US with government-mandated securities filing disclosures and the Toxic Release Inventory (TRI) of the Environmental Protection Agency (EPA).

Cohen, Fenn and Naimon took various environmental measures for each firm including the number of Superfund sites the firm had, the number of compliance penalties, volume of toxic chemical releases, number and volume of oil spills, number and volume of chemical spills and number of environmental litigation proceedings. They controlled for firm size and matched companies according to industry, creating two portfolios, one of 'high polluters' and one of 'low polluters'. The two portfolios were then compared on a number of financial indicators, return on assets, return on equity and total returns to normal shareholders, between 1987 and 1989.

They found that in more than 80 per cent of the portfolio comparisons the low pollution portfolio outperforms the high pollution portfolio and concluded that it does not appear that investors who construct a balanced portfolio of good environmental performers will pay a penalty in terms of market performance. They optimistically stated: 'as environmental issues take on greater importance we would expect the relationship to become even stronger'.

A significant weakness in this type of research lies in ascertaining the direction of causation of the effect, a fact acknowledged by researchers themselves:

For example, a finding that good environmental performance is correlated with high earnings does not necessarily mean that firms who improve their environmental performance will also improve their earnings. It is possible that causation runs the other way, that firms are good environmental citizens because they are financially strong and can afford to be good citizens.

[Cohen, Scott and Naimon 1995]

It may also be that greener firms are more profitable because they are more efficient and, as Sir John Harvey-Jones stated when he was chairman of ICI, because they are producing more and more with less and less. A lack of environmental time series data has so far precluded further investigation of the direction of causation.

Hart and Ahuja at Michigan University also used data from the Investor Responsibility Research Center but concentrated on emissions volumes as an indicator of firm environmental performance. They devised a value for emissions reduction using the ratio of reported emissions in pounds, to the company's revenues in thousands of dollars. The change in emissions from 1988 to 1989 for each firm was set against return on sales, return on assets and return on equity.

Hart and Ahuja controlled for a number of potential underlying effects including research intensity, advertising intensity, capital and leverage. A value for the relevant industry average performance was also included. A set of hypotheses on the relationship between emissions reduction and operating and financial performance were tested. These were: a) that performance would be related to emissions reduction with a time-lag of at least one year, and b) that emissions reduction would enhance the performance more for firms with high emissions levels than for firms with low emissions levels.

Results from the regressions carried out by the authors suggest that 'efforts to prevent pollution and reduce emissions appear to drop to the bottom line within 1–2 years after initiation'. All three financial indicators show significant improvements when efforts to reduce pollution are made. Interestingly Hart and Ahuja found that return on equity takes longer to show an impact than either return on sales or return on assets. This, they suggested, was due in part to emissions reduction affecting the firm's cost of capital as the market becomes aware of the firm's environmental performance. On the second hypothesis they comment:

As expected, the biggest benefits accrue to the 'high polluters' where there are plenty of low-cost improvements to be made. It appears that the closer a firm gets to 'zero pollution' the more expensive it gets, as further reductions mean rising capital and technology investments. Yet the results also show that the marginal costs of reducing emissions do not exceed marginal benefits.

[Hart and Ahuja 1994]

One of the few attempts made in the UK to link environmental and financial performance was unpublished research carried out by Poole and Mansley on behalf of Nottingham County Council in July 1996. They took 17 companies which had been researched by the Jupiter Environmental Research Unit and matched each company in this 'green' sample with a company of similar profile from the Financial Times All-Share listing chosen by random stratified sampling. Comparing total returns over a period of five years, they found that in 1992 and 1993 the green basket of companies performed significantly better than the inferior environmental group. The reverse conclusion held true for 1995 while no statistically significant difference was observed in 1994.

The study went on to investigate the hypothesis that the difference in financial performance between green and dirty companies is larger in industrial sectors where environmental issues are of greater concern. Sector Environmental Impact Severity scores produced by the European Union (EU)/European Free Trade Association (EFTA) were used to distinguish between sectors. No evidence was found to support this hypothesis. However the authors suggest that the results should be interpreted with a degree of caution due to the small sample size.

Market Reaction to Environmental Performance

Studies of the impact of environmental events, such as fines or large environmental investments, on firm share price generally support the idea of market awareness of environmental performance. Market theory holds that the share price of a firm reflects all available information and this may include environmental information which often involves significant financial saving or expenditure.

A paper by Hamilton (1995) suggests that the share prices of polluting corporations in the US tended to fall after the EPA reported adversely on their pollution performance. In the UK, Piesse (1992) used three case studies from the oil industry to examine the effect of environmental spending on share price performance. The share prices of Conoco, Du Pont and Shell were investigated and compared against industry indexes, during and after major environmental 'events'.

In the case of Conoco, a major programme to reduce toxic emissions and prevent oil spills was announced in April 1990. This involved expenditure of $50 million per year and included the building of two double hulled tankers costing 15 per cent more than conventional tankers. One might expect the shares to be discounted in comparison to the rest of the sector since no legislation forced the expenditure and such spending could be identified by the markets as unnecessary. In fact Piesse concluded: '... the announcement of the environmental spending programme did not significantly discount the share price, and may have increased it relative to the rest of the sector' (1992).

Data presented on Exxon suggested that in 1989, in the weeks following the *Exxon Valdez* disaster, in which significant amounts of crude oil were spilled in an environmentally sensitive area, Exxon's share price was discounted heavily in relation to a basket of peer group companies. Similarly when Shell were fined £1 million for a spill of oil into the Mersey River in 1989, Piesse found that:

...at least temporarily, the markets felt that the expected value of Shell Transport's earnings stream was lower than that of the RDS (comparator) group. The discrepancy in values was 20p per share or £670 million. This amount is far greater than the actual cost of the cleanup and the fine, and demonstrates that even small environmental accidents can detrimentally affect a company's share price.

[Piesse 1992]

A key link in the process between 'event' and share price move are the financial analysts. Spencer-Cooke (1994) finds evidence to suggest that this group may be starting to look carefully at the financial implications of environmental performance. The emphasis is very much on the financial risks or opportunities that a firm's environmental strategy can entail.

Spencer-Cooke asked respondents to explain the drop in a company's share price which occurred following an incident at one of its plants. Reasons given were concern about a hit on earnings through lost business due to poor company image, or lost production capacity and the threat of higher insurance costs and potential fines. These are financial realities rather than high-flown green rhetoric and their incidence is likely to increase. As environmental information flow improves, analysts, companies and green activists will become more adept at the pricing of environmental performance so that it can be combined with other relevant market information. In the same report, Spencer-Cooke found that 90 per cent of those surveyed declared that 'links existed between the environmental and financial performance of a company'.

Green Portfolios

Portfolio analysis has been carried out by business analysts and strategy consultants for many years. At the business strategy level the portfolio framework can help firms evaluate the impact of specific products and can support decisions regarding product development and marketing. At the corporate strategy level, the technique can assist firms in identifying and evaluating acquisition and divestiture candidates and in evaluating a company's competitive position within its primary industry environment.

Portfolio analysis has traditionally only involved the use of economic indicators such as relative growth or market share. However Ilinitch and Schaltegger (1995) have suggested that environmental performance measures might be integrated into such models to produce an ecologically-oriented portfolio matrix. This could be used by analysts to evaluate the impact of environmental actions on various products when used at the business level, or used by holding companies and industry analysts to compare the impact of environmental performance on company economic performance relative to its competitors.

As with environmental managerial accounting described in the last chapter, the internal use of the portfolio matrix by firms requires the use of detailed information on environmental impacts associated with the various processes and products in the company's operation. The calculation of 'pollution units' is offered by Ilinitch and Schaltegger as one way of providing the relevant information. In ecological accounting, pollution units are calculated by multiplying the discharges of toxic substances to the air, land and water by a pollutant-specific weighting factor derived from environmental regulation standards.

Clearly few companies will have an environmental information system capable of gathering this data. However Ciba Geigy is one that does and it is used by Ilinitch and Schaltegger as an example of the practical application of green portfolio matrix for internal strategic planning.

An existing detailed effluent inventory was used by Ciba Geigy to investigate the environmental and related economic impacts of a change in pigment production technology. They found that the changes enhanced the economic position of the pigment due to production efficiency and product quality improving. However they also discovered that this change led to an increase in the number of pollution units because more electrical power was required per unit of production and total sales increased. Later changes in the technology, improved both economic and environmental performance so that the pigment ultimately moved to a greener and more profitable position. Ciba Geigy were able to benefit from analysing the impact of the production changes on both the financial and environmental performance of the company. By using this approach managers can more easily recognise the opportunities and threats presented by a particular product or process and change the budgeting emphasis accordingly.

The authors also profiled an example of the use of the green portfolio matrix to perform competitor analysis of six multi national chemical companies. They used data available from the US EPA's TRI to examine the relationship between the economic attractiveness of a company and its environmental impact. The companies analysed were: American Cyanamid, Ciba Geigy Corporation, Dow, Du Pont, ICI and Monsanto. The authors noted that there were problems with the economic analysis as sales growth and profitability for the entire industry declined between 1989–90 (the period of study) but nonetheless concluded that:

> *In matrix terms American Cyanamid was moving toward the 'dirty dog' position during this time period, while Du Pont was moving toward the green star position. Dow's move toward a dirtier position was accompanied by strong sales growth yet a loss in profitability, while Du Pont's move toward a greener position was accompanied by its ability to maintain profit and sales growth. Ciba-Geigy and ICI remained the greenest firms over the two-year time frame, without experiencing extreme loss of position in sales growth or profitability relative to their competitors.*
>
> [Ilinitch and Schaltegger 1995]

A more recent portfolio paper, *Environmental Screens and Portfolio Performance: A Comparative Analysis* (Clough 1997) looked at a portfolio of firms which had been screened for environmental attributes like those used by green and ethical investment funds. Clough found that, at a minimum, an environmental screen does not degrade financial performance as measured by a portfolio's total return.

Conclusion

Existing studies suggest that there is a link between environmental and financial performance, particularly the quantitative studies carried out in the US. Studies based on both company financial results and market valuations have shown evidence for such a link. There appears to be little evidence of firms paying a financial penalty for good environmental performance, as long as investments made to achieve this are taken with the same care as other capital and operating investment decisions.

CHAPTER 3
METHODOLOGY

Scope and Research Objectives

The study involved the examination of the historical financial results from 51 companies from the Approved List of the Jupiter Environmental Research Unit (JERU). These data were compared to the financial data of a number of companies whose environmental performance was unknown. All companies are UK based and are listed on the London Stock Exchange. The objective of the study was to examine empirically the relationship between the environmental and historical financial performance of these companies.

As discussed in the previous chapter, one of the main reasons for the paucity of research on the link between environmental and financial performance, is the lack of structured and comparable environmental data for companies. This is particularly the case in the UK where an emphasis on voluntary disclosure has meant information of varying quality and quantity especially where individual company pollution records are concerned:

> *Until recently, companies were not required to disclose in their corporate accounts, details of research and development expenditure, either regarding the nature of the research or the areas of operations affected, and a fair amount of research and development is based around safety and reducing pollution levels. Only the aggregate emission needed to be reported, and this gave a minimal amount of information, both to existing or potential shareholders, and to researchers.*

[Piesse 1992]

One good source of such data, however, is the research teams of the various green investment funds that have been launched since the early 1980s. Some funds specialise in ethical and social performance and others, like the Ecology Fund of the Jupiter International Green Investment Trust (JIGIT), which was the first authorised green investment trust to be launched in Europe, specifically evaluate the environmental performance of companies in addition to some ethical screening criteria. The JIGIT mission is:

> *To provide its shareholders with long term capital appreciation, together with growing income, by investing in companies that are responding positively to the challenge of environmental sustainability and are making a commitment to social well-being.*

[JIGIT Annual Report 1995]

One of the key reasons that ethical and green investment funds have grown by 26 per cent since 1994 (Holden Meehan 1996) may be that, due to the voluntary and self-regulated nature of much of the environmental management practiced by companies, it has become possible to identify, and invest in, the leaders (JERU 1995).

Assessing Environmental Performance

The JERU Approved List of companies for their Ecology Fund was used by this study to give a sample of companies meeting best environmental practice in a variety of sectors. Companies on the Approved List meet certain standards regarding environmental performance and have passed the assessment process used by JERU. Companies are chosen for research purposes as potential candidates for the Approved List by JERU in collaboration with the fund manager; however the companies on the Approved List are chosen purely on their environmental merit. Of the total 105 UK companies on the Approved List, only about half will be in the investment portfolio at any one time, depending on their current or projected financial performance.

The JERU environmental assessment process uses both negative and positive screening criteria with the emphasis on the positive. The negative approach applies to seven activities: the alcoholic drinks trade, animal testing, armaments, gambling, nuclear power generation, publication of pornographic material and tobacco. Companies deriving more than 10 per cent will fail at this stage and will not be included on the Approved List. If a company is involved in any of these activities and derives less than 10 per cent of turnover from them, it would have to show an outstanding contribution to sustainable development in other respects to be considered for investment by the Green Fund. An example of this would be the water treatment sector. A number of otherwise excellent companies sell ultrapure water to nuclear power plants. Under negative screening these companies could be barred from ethical funds. However Jupiter believes that some companies in this sector have made more important positive contributions to sustainable development – by improving aquatic environments and raising the efficiency of water use.

The more rigorous positive assessment involves examination of the complete environmental performance of the company. An integrated, systematic and sustained performance by the company is considered particularly important and this is primarily assessed by experienced personnel through dialogue with companies, company visits and face-to-face meetings.

A complete assessment of a potential addition to the Approved List would include an analysis of company literature, a response to a Standard Questionnaire, dialogue with the company and input, perhaps from informed commentators who may have specialised industrial knowledge relating to the company under assessment. Wherever possible the research team will also undertake a visit of the company's operations (JERU 1995).

JERU is assisted in its research by the Jupiter Environmental Advisory Committee, consisting of eminent environmentalists, which it meets on a formal basis every three months. The Advisory Committee provides advice on assessment techniques, ensuring these stay at the forefront of current best practice; guidance on questions of an ethical nature; and specific recommendations on investment and disinvestment in particular companies.

There have been numerous attempts to develop quantitative techniques for enabling comparative studies of corporate performance. However, to date no widely adopted techniques exist for UK companies. The assessment of company environmental performance by JERU appears to be amongst the most rigorous, comparable and consistent of any such assessments. The Holden Meehan, *Independent Guide to Ethical and Green Investment Funds* (1996), rated the Jupiter Ecology Fund against similar funds, as first, both for the emphasis it places on environmental companies as investments, and also for the resources applied to screening. These factors suggest that the results of the JERU company environmental assessments are the best data source for this study.

Box 3.1: Summary of the Jupiter Evironmental Research Unit
Environmental Criteria for Assessment

Beneficial products and services
Jupiter's Green Funds actively seek to invest in companies that manufacture products or provide services that have an environmental or social benefit.

Environmental technology manufacturers
Examples include companies which produce emissions control equipment (eg water filters and airborne particulate traps) or renewable energy technologies (eg photovoltaic cells).

Healthcare products and services
Products may include equipment for diagnostics, sterilisation and waste handling for use in surgeries, homecare or hospitals. Services may include the provision of homecare and nursing facilities.

Telecommunications and Information Technologies
These sectors are favoured by the Green Funds because of their potential roles in addressing transport and the consumption of printed matter.

Transport
Public transport companies are favoured by the Green Funds because of their contribution to reducing congestion and airborne pollution.

Other products
Companies which provide other socially beneficial products such as educational and safety equipment may be favoured by the Green Funds, as may companies which produce the most environmentally preferable model of a given product.

Disclosure
JERU supports greater transparency and openness about the environmental activities of companies, while placing emphasis on the quantification of the information that is disclosed and a company's annual performance in relation to stated targets.

Greenhouse gases
Although global warming is far from understood, it is expected to disrupt weather patterns. The Green Funds recognise this threat and favour companies which minimise emissions of greenhouse gases.

Ozone depleting substances
The Green Funds invest in companies which are moving towards a total cessation of their use of ozone depleting substances and which are, in the interim, actively reducing leakage.

Packaging and Labelling
JERU favours companies which are actively seeking to minimise their packing waste by reducing, reusing or recycling and labelling packaging products.

Sustainable agriculture
Only companies which are committed to sustainable agricultural practices, high standards of animal welfare and low chemical input will be added to the Approved List.

Sustainable resource use
There is considerable concern about the unsustainable 'mining' of natural resources such as old open growth forests and wild fish stocks. The Green Funds favour companies that operate best practice with respect to the sustainable use of these resources.

[Source: *The Assessment Process for Green Investment, JERU, 1997 (Appendix A)*]

**Box 3.2: Summary of the Jupiter Environmental Research Unit
Environmental Management Criteria**

JERU not only seeks to find those companies that already have comprehensive environmental management systems in place but also those companies that are committed to continuously improving their performance by systematically implementing environmentally sound management procedures. Although companies demonstrate their commitment to environmental protection in different ways, key indicators include the following:

Corporate Environmental Policy
Companies that publish environmental policy statements committing themselves to substantive action will be favoured by JERU particularly when the policy is effectively communicated to stakeholders.

Environmental Management Systems
For inclusion in the Green Fund, companies are not obliged to follow any particular model of environmental management system. However an undertaking to apply the International Standards Organisation's Environmental Management System (ISO14001), or the European Community's Eco-management and Audit Scheme (EMAS), is regarded as a good indicator of the structured commitment to environmental management that JERU seeks.

Monitoring Environmental Impact
How well a company monitors its own environmental performance. The principal tool for such monitoring is the environmental audit. To be useful audits should be regular and conducted, or verified, by a third party.

Trading Partner Assessments
How rigorously a company assesses the environmental performance of its trading partners. This principally applies to suppliers but can also cover the performance of contractors. JERU attaches great significance to the 'cradle-to-grave' approach to assessment and therefore favours companies that have considered the impact of all their operations, from raw material extraction through to final disposal. The Unit assesses the mechanisms – such as questionnaires, audits or dialogue – that companies use in their supply chain scrutiny.

Energy Efficiency
How effective a company is at reducing its energy consumption. As one of the simplest methods of minimising environmental impact, this provides JERU with an indicator of corporate commitment to environmental improvement. In particular, the Research Unit enquires whether companies have recognised the principle of 'continuous improvement' by setting continuous improvement targets for energy efficiency.

Responsibility
Whether environmental responsibility rests with a main board director and how much of that person's time is spent on environmental issues. The Research Unit also enquires whether there is a formal hierarchy of environmental accountability throughout the company.

Environmental Communication
How fully employees are informed about, and involved in, environmental issues, and the extent of the provision of training relating to the environment.

Legal compliance
Compliance with regulations is regarded as a minimum standard rather than a target for companies within the green portfolio. Accordingly JERU assesses whether the company is, or has been, the subject of prosecution or litigation, or has otherwise attracted adverse attention from regulatory bodies.

[Source: *The Assessment Process for Green Investment, JERU, 1997 (Appendix A)*]

Analysis of Data

The study is divided by industry sector as defined by the All Share listing of the *Financial Times*. These sectors are:

- building materials and merchants;
- healthcare;
- engineering;
- electrical and electronic equipment;
- support services;
- food retailers;
- general retailers; and
- paper, packaging and printing.

On the subject of environmental assessment at a sector level *The Assessment Process for Green Investment* (Jupiter Environmental Research Unit 1997) states:

> *JERU believes that Sector Assessments are an important part of the positive approach to green investment, because within all sectors of industry there is scope for companies to improve their environmental performance and those that are 'best in class' should be recognised and encouraged to improve. Sector leaders will be added to the list provided they do not breach the negative criteria.*

The JERU Approved List which is used here as a green sample will therefore contain the best environmental performers within a sector.

The optimal data set for this study would also include a list of companies investigated by Jupiter and found to be low environmental performers within a sector. This would then be compared with companies in the same sector from the Approved List. As such a list is not available, the data for comparison are taken from any other companies on the UK Stock Exchange which have not been selected by JERU for inclusion on the Approved List. It is assumed that the environmental performance of these companies is inferior to that of the companies on the Approved List.

A number of companies on the complete Approved List were excluded from analysis on the grounds that historical financial data was unavailable, as they had not been listed on the London Stock Exchange for the years analysed.

Stage 1 Analysis

For each company on the Approved List analysed, between three and five companies of similar profile from the same sector were identified for comparative purposes. This gave a 'green' sample – the companies on the Approved List, and a 'non-green' sample – other companies of similar profile. The sector that a company was included in was defined by the All Share listing of the Financial Times.

Stage 2 Analysis

In order to further test the robustness of any relationship, the data were subjected to a second analysis.

From the set of non-green companies of similar profile identified in the first stage, the company which showed the best financial performance was selected. This single non-green company was compared to its matching green company on the same financial indicators over the same time period as in the first stage. This contrasts with the first stage because the financial results for the best performing company of similar profile were taken instead of an average result for a number of companies. By performing Stage 2 of the analysis an element of financial pre-selection is introduced in the non-green sample. This was done in order to test the strength of any relationship found at Stage 1.

An overview of the analysis is shown in Figure 3.1.

Financial Indicators

The financial performance indicators chosen reflect accounting returns through the use of return on capital employed and return on equity. Return on Capital Employed (ROCE) is included as a measure of the efficiency of the capital employed in producing income. Return on Equity (ROE) is a measure of the performance of the company relative to shareholder investment.

Profile Characteristics

The profile characteristics selected were: subsector and turnover, capitalisation, capital expenditure per share and the percentage of export turnover in 1995.

Subsector was chosen to control for effects specific to the operations of particular industries. These may be internal effects such as differing processes which thus use different raw materials and produce different wastes. There may also be differences in external pressures such as public perception and applicable legislation. Turnover and capitalisation were chosen to allow for effects of size such as economies of scale and potential for growth. Capital expenditure per share gives some indication of the scale of recent investment by the firm and the percentage of export turnover was chosen to control for differing legislative intensities and emphases outside the UK.

For each green company and each non-green company, the two financial indicators, return on equity (ROE) and return on capital employed (ROCE) were used to give an indication of firm financial performance. These were taken for each year between 1992–5, and an average for the four years was also calculated. An average of the values for the 3–5 non-green companies of similar profile for ROE and ROCE was found. This was to reduce the possibility of other factors affecting the results. These figures were taken from the July 1996 edition of *Company REFS (Really Essential Financial Statistics)*.

The results for each sector were then collated and summarised and a statistical 't' test used to test for significance. Factors that may affect statistical significance include the number of companies analysed in the sector, and whether there are any individual results which differ greatly from the norm.

Figure 3.1: Analysis of Environmental and Financial Performance

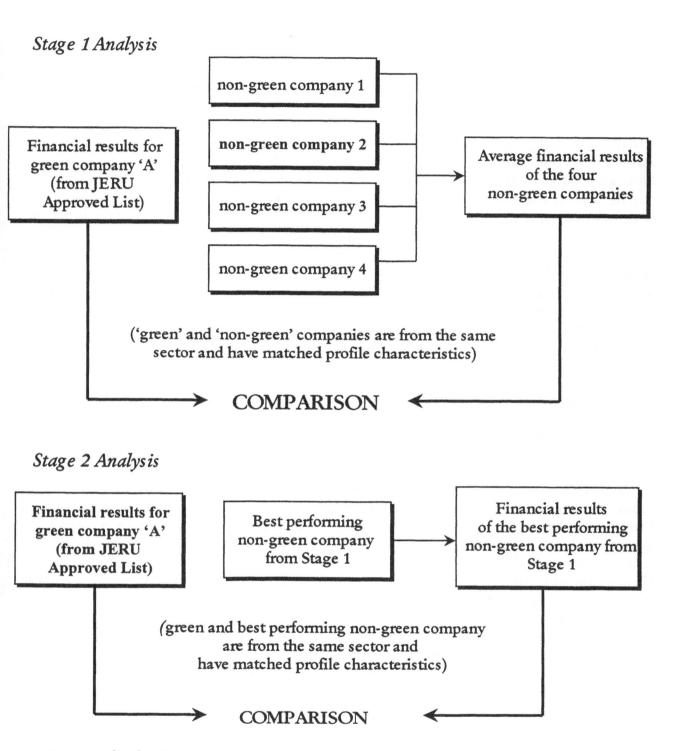

Stage 1 Analysis

Financial results for green company 'A' (from JERU Approved List)	non-green company 1
	non-green company 2
	non-green company 3
	non-green company 4

Average financial results of the four non-green companies

('green' and 'non-green' companies are from the same sector and have matched profile characteristics)

COMPARISON

Stage 2 Analysis

Financial results for green company 'A' (from JERU Approved List)

Best performing non-green company from Stage 1

Financial results of the best performing non-green company from Stage 1

(green and best performing non-green company are from the same sector and have matched profile characteristics)

COMPARISON

Stages 1 and 2 of analysis are carried out for each year from 1992 to 1996 and for an average of those years

Profile characteristics: *Subsector*
Turnover
Capitalisation
Capital expenditure per share
Percentage of export turnover

Financial indicators: *Return on Capital Employed*
Return on Equity

Constraints and Limitations

Some of the companies in the non-green sample of this study may actually have superior environmental performance to those on the Approved List but have not come to JERU's notice or have been discounted on the ethical criteria that JERU set. It is possible to imagine, for example, an alcoholic drinks company which has good environmental performance relative to its competitors but which would be precluded from the Approved List by the fact that it derives more than 10 per cent of its income from alcohol.

More generally, public perception may preclude green funds from investing in sectors such as mining and chemicals which, even though they may have clear leaders in terms of environmental management, are perceived as being intrinsically harmful. For instance, although Rio Tinto mining company, which produces a stand-alone environmental report, submits to independent audits, spends significant sums on rehabilitation and is listed by UNI Storebrand of Norway in its Environmental Value Fund, it is unlikely that a UK based green fund would feel able to do the same due to local pressures generated by controversial London based annual general meetings of recent years. Thus the diversity of sector analysis is constrained.

The term 'environmental performance' is used many times in this report. As Andrea Spencer-Cooke comments:

> *There is an intrinsic limitation in dealing with concepts such as 'corporate environmental performance' and 'environmental information', since there exist at present no generally accepted definitions for these terms.*

[Spencer-Cooke 1994]

Unless judged on directly comparable and quantitative indicators, there will be an element of subjectivity in the designation of companies as 'good' or 'bad' environmental performers. Personal judgements will assign differing values to the same environmental impacts, and will mean that the environmental issues affected by those impacts, for example ozone depletion, acid rain or air pollution, are ranked in differing ways with respect to their importance. Having said this, the rigour of the JERU assessment is well respected and the input of the Advisory Committee ensures a wide range of perspectives.

In some sectors it was difficult to find enough companies of similar profile as comparator companies. This was especially the case in the support services sector where a number of subsectors are listed in a single sector.

It is often unclear when companies may have implemented environmental programmes. This precludes any investigation of the effect of implementation on the historical financial data.

CHAPTER 4
RESULTS

Presentation of Results

The results from the eight sectors are presented in Tables 4.1–4.32 and are summarised in pie chart format in Figures 4.1–4.18.

Presentation of the Data in Tables 4.1-4.32

The first two tables (4.1 and 4.2) summarise the results for all companies across all sectors. The rest of the tabular data is presented by sector, with four tables for each sector. These are return on capital employed at Stages 1 and 2, and return on equity at Stages 1 and 2.

Stage 1 Tables
Stage 1 tables refer to the comparison of the green companies to the average results of 3–5 other companies of similar profile in the same sector and not on the Approved list. There are five rows in the table each referring to one green company in this sector. If, when compared to the average results of the non-green companies, the green company does better, then 'G' is recorded. If the non-green average is better, then 'N' is recorded.

Stage 2 Tables
Stage 2 tables show the results of the second stage of analysis. Similarly to Stage 1, the green values are the mean of the results for the companies which have been taken from the JERU Approved list. However, the non-green values in the Stage 2 tables are the results for the best financially performing company, from those of similar profile identified in Stage 1.

Example A: Explanation of the Tabular Presentation of Data

All tables follow the format described below except Tables 4.1 and 4.2 which present a summary of the results for all of the companies analysed, across all sectors.

Building Materials & Merchants

Number of companies analysed: Five

Example: Stage 1: Return on Capital Employed

1992	1993	1994	1995	1996	1992–96(ave)	
						Year data is taken from, final column shows ave. of 1992–6
G	G	G	G	G	G	Green firm 1 compared with ave. of non-green firms
G	G	G	N	N	G	Green firm 2
N	N	N	N	N	N	Green firm 3
G	G	G	G	G	G	etc
G	G	G	G	G	G	

'G' recorded if green results are better, 'N' for better non-green results.

Average results of the **green** companies are significantly better than those of their **non-green** rivals in this year
Average results of the **green** companies are better than the **non-green** companies, but the data fails a statistical test
Average results of the **non-green** companies are better than the results of the **green** companies

(Stage 1 is repeated for Return on Equity and is shown in a similar tabular format).

Example: Stage 2: Return on Capital Employed

1992	1993	1994	1995	1996	1992–96(ave)	
G	G	G	G	G	G	Year data is taken from, final column shows ave. of 1992–6
N	N	G	N	N	N	**Green** firm 1 against **best performer** of **non-green** firms
N	N	N	N	N	N	**Green** company 2
G	G	G	G	N	G	**Green** company 3
G	G	G	G	G	G	etc

'G' recorded if green results are better, 'N' for better non-green results.

Average results of the *green* companies are significantly better than those of their *non-green* rivals in this year
Average results of the *green* companies are better than the *non-green* companies, but the data fails a statistical test
Average results of the *non-green* companies are better than the results of the *green* companies

(Stage 2 is repeated for Return on equity and is shown in a similar tabular format).

Presentation of the Data in Figures 4.1–4.18

The pie charts are a summary of Tables 4.1–4.32, and show the results of the direct comparisons of the financial results between 1992 and 1996, and the average of those years, for green and non-green companies at Stage 1 and Stage 2 of the analysis (see Methodology for definition of Stage 1 and Stage 2).

Example B: Explanation of the Pie Chart Presentation of Data

Example Stage 2: General Retailers

75%

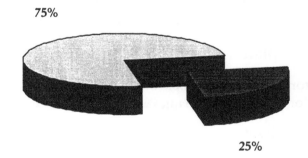

25%

Example B shows the sum of all comparisons made between green and non-green building companies for the years 1992–6 (and the average of those years) at Stage 1 of the analysis. if the financial results of a company were better than the average of the non-green companies in a particular year then one 'point' is scored to green companies. If the reverse is true a point is scored to non-green companies. A point equates to a 'G' or 'N' recorded in the tables (see Example A).

For instance in Example B, 75 per cent of points were scored by green companies and 25 per cent by non-green companies.

Results

All Companies

Number of green companies analysed: 50

Table 4.1: Stage 1: All Companies

	1992		1993		1994		1995		1996		1992–6 (ave)	
	green	non-green	green	non-green	green	non-green	green	non-green	green	non-green	green	non-green
ROCE (%)	23.22	12.78	26.80	12.23	24.93	13.63	25.08	16.42	24.96	16.84	24.96	14.38
ROE (%)	19.49	5.37	20.92	4.00	18.42	7.71	19.2	12.28	18.40	13.66	13.66	8.6

Table 4.2: Stage 2: All Companies

	1992		1993		1994		1995		1996		1992–6 (ave)	
	green	non-green	green	non-green	green	non-green	green	non-green	green	non-green	green	non-green
ROCE (%)	23.22	22.73	26.80	22.92	24.93	24.64	25.08	27.05	24.96	26.12	24.92	24.69
ROE (%)	19.49	16.85	20.92	18.54	18.42	21.59	19.2	25.33	18.40	27.96	19.29	22.05

Shading indicates that the average financial results of the green companies are better than those of the non-green companies

The figures in tables 4.1 and 4.2 were obtained by taking the financial results for all companies, across all sectors and finding the average.

Tables 4.1 and 4.2 show the green companies outperforming the non-green companies in all of the years the data were examined. When Stage 2 analysis is performed the green companies still do well, although in 1995 and 1996 the non-green companies have the better financial performance.

Electrical & Electronic Equipment

Number of green companies analysed: Eight

Table 4.3: Stage 1: Return on Capital Employed

1992	1993	1994	1995	1996	1992–96 (ave)
G	G	G	G	G	G
G	G	G	G	G	G
G	G	G	G	G	G
G	G	G	G	G	G
N	G	G	G	G	G
G	G	G	G	G	G
G	G	N	N	N	N
G	G	G	N	N	G
G	G	G	G	G	G

Table 4.4: Stage 1: Return on Equity

1992	1993	1994	1995	1996	1992–96 (ave)
G	G	G	N	N	N
G	G	G	G	G	G
G	G	G	G	G	G
N	G	G	G	N	G
G	G	G	G	G	G
G	G	G	G	G	G
N	G	N	N	N	N
G	G	G	G	N	G
G	G	G	G	G	G

Table 4.5: Stage 2: Return on Capital Employed

1992	1993	1994	1995	1996	1992–96 (ave)
N	N	N	N	N	N
N	G	G	N	N	N
G	G	G	G	G	G
N	G	G	N	N	N
N	N	N	G	G	G
G	G	G	G	G	G
G	G	N	N	N	N
G	G	N	N	N	N
G	G	G	G	G	G

Table 4.6: Stage 2: Return on Equity

1992	1993	1994	1995	1996	1992–96 (ave)
N	N	N	N	N	N
N	N	G	N	N	N
G	G	G	G	G	G
N	G	G	N	N	N
G	N	N	G	G	G
G	G	G	G	G	G
N	G	N	N	N	N
G	G	G	N	N	G
G	G	N	G	G	G

▨ Average results of the *green* companies are significantly better than those of their *non-green* rivals in this year
▨ Average results of the *green* companies are better than the *non-green* companies, but the data fails a statistical test
☐ Average results of the *non-green* companies are better than the results of the *green* companies

At Stage 1, as shown by Tables 4.13 and 4.14, green companies perform significantly better than non-green in terms of both return on equity and return on capital employed. The results at Stage 2 favour the non-green companies in most years. This is a similar sector to the healthcare sector as it has many new companies with unproven technology, which, once confirmed as being commercially viable, disproportionately affects returns. We see the same good performance at Stage 2 in the early years by green companies as in the healthcare sector, with these being overshadowed by the huge returns of the electronic 'hot' stocks.

The electronics industry has historically been perceived as being environmentally low impact. The discovery of serious pollution and groundwater contamination in Silicon Valley and the increase in the proportion of electronics waste going to landfill, has recently given cause for concern. Important environmental issues for this industry include energy consumption, ozone depletion through the use of CFCs in production, and hazardous and non-hazardous wastes. The production of a single semiconductor chip weighing 10 grams is a process involving 400 steps, 28 kilograms of chemicals and 11 kilograms of neutralising sodium hydroxide. (O'Connor 1994). A study by the US Microelectronics Computer Technology Corporation estimated that it takes 33,000 litres of water to make one computer workstation. Clearly these are issues that need to be addressed by the industry if it is to tackle the concept of sustainable development.

Microvitec is a JERU Approved list company and is part of the above analysis. This British company manufactures colour terminals for the computer industry. It has a stated intention to work towards BS 7750 accreditation and is taking initiatives in energy consumption, recycling and packaging take-back. It is committed to reducing the power use of its monitors. Peek plc, which manufactures hand-held computers for traffic and field data systems, is another company in the green sample above. They intend to reduce costs by cutting energy consumption by 5 per cent and will phase out CFCs by adopting new processes.

The benefits of such efforts will become more apparent as companies introduce environmental criteria into computer hardware purchase decisions, as landfill costs increase and as consumer concern rises about the disposal of products that they may be upgrading every few years. There are real difficulties in recycling complex multi-material products such as televisions or computers, however the designation of electronics waste as a priority waste stream by the European Commission is likely to concentrate future waste management efforts by this industry.

Engineering

Number of green companies analysed: Seven

Table 4.7: Stage 1: Return on Capital Employed

1992	1993	1994	1995	1996	1992–96 (ave)
G	G	G	G	G	G
G	G	G	G	G	G
G	G	G	G	G	G
G	G	G	G	G	G
G	G	G	G	G	G
G	N	N	N	N	N
G	G	G	G	G	G

Table 4.8: Stage 1: Return on Equity

1992	1993	1994	1995	1996	1992–96 (ave)
G	G	G	G	G	G
G	G	G	G	G	G
G	G	G	N	N	G
G	G	G	G	G	G
G	G	N	G	G	G
G	G	G	N	N	G
N	N	N	N	N	N

Table 4.9: Stage 2: Return on Capital Employed

1992	1993	1994	1995	1996	1992-96 (ave)
G	G	G	G	G	G
N	N	G	G	G	G
G	G	G	N	N	G
G	G	G	G	G	G
G	G	G	G	G	G
N	N	N	N	N	N
G	G	N	N	G	G

Table 4.10: Stage 2: Return on Equity

1992	1993	1994	1995	1996	1992-96 (ave)
G	G	G	G	G	G
G	G	G	G	G	G
G	N	N	N	N	N
G	G	N	N	N	N
G	G	N	N	G	N
N	N	N	N	N	N
N	N	N	N	G	N

Average results of the **green** companies are significantly better than those of their **non-green** rivals in this year
Average results of the **green** companies are better than the **non-green** companies, but the data fails a statistical test
Average results of the **non-green** companies are better than the results of the **green** companies

The engineering sector shows the most significant results of any sector investigated. Only the return on equity comparison in 1995 at Stage 1 (Table 4.8), appears not to come down significantly in favour of the green firms. At Stage 2, having taken the best financially performing firm from the non-green sample in Stage 1, all of the comparisons made for return on capital employed (Table 4.9) appear to favour the green firms.

This is a diverse sector in terms of products and processes which suggests that the green firms employ a wide variety of solutions to environmental challenges encountered. It is likely that in the engineering sector, more so than in the retail sector, for example, there are good opportunities to use measures such as energy efficiency, water saving and reuse of materials to make real, positive impact on the bottom line cost of production.

Healthcare

Number of green companies analysed: Seven

Table 4.11: Stage 1: Return on Capital Employed

1992	1993	1994	1995	1996	1992–96 (ave)
G	G	G	G	G	G
N	G	N	N	N	N
G	G	G	G	G	G
G	G	G	G	G	G
N	N	N	N	N	N
G	G	G	G	G	G
N	G	G	G	G	G

Table 4.12: Stage 1: Return on Equity

1992	1993	1994	1995	1996	1992–96 (ave)
G	G	G	G	G	G
G	G	N	N	N	N
G	G	G	G	G	G
G	G	G	G	G	G
N	N	N	N	N	N
G	G	G	G	G	G
N	N	G	G	G	G

Table 4.13: Stage 2: Return on Capital Employed

1992	1993	1994	1995	1996	1992–96 (ave)
N	N	N	N	N	N
N	N	N	N	N	N
G	G	G	G	G	G
G	G	G	G	G	G
N	N	N	N	N	N
G	G	G	G	G	G
N	G	G	G	G	G

Table 4.14: Stage 2: Return on Equity

1992	1993	1994	1995	1996	1992–96 (ave)
G	G	G	G	G	G
G	G	N	N	N	N
G	G	G	G	G	G
G	G	G	G	G	G
N	N	N	N	N	N
G	G	G	G	G	G
N	N	G	G	G	G

Average results of the **green** companies are significantly better than those of their **non-green** rivals in this year
Average results of the **green** companies are better than the **non-green** companies, but the data fails a statistical test
Average results of the **non-green** companies are better than the results of the **green** companies

The results for green companies in the healthcare sector appear to be better than those of the non-green companies, often significantly. However, in the more stringent analysis of Stage 2, the non-green results are better.

The healthcare sector contains a number of very new companies involved in cutting-edge medical technology. These stocks, like those in the information technology and biotechnology sectors, often perform averagely until the potential of a product or service is fully realised, when performances, especially in terms of return on equity, become very strong in relation to other more mature companies. The green sample contained fewer of the new stocks and this may explain both the relatively strong performance of the green companies in earlier years, and also the poor performance of the green companies, as the strong performers were hand-picked at Stage 2.

Support Services

Number of green companies analysed: Seven

Table 4.15: Stage 1: Return on Capital Employed

1992	1993	1994	1995	1996	1992–96 (ave)
G	N	G	G	G	G
G	G	G	G	N	G
G	G	G	G	G	G
G	G	G	G	G	G
G	G	G	G	G	G
N	G	N	N	N	N
G	G	G	G	G	G

Table 4.16: Stage 1: Return on Equity

1992	1993	1994	1995	1996	1992–96 (ave)
G	G	G	G	G	G
G	G	G	G	N	G
G	G	G	G	G	G
G	G	G	G	N	G
N	G	G	G	G	G
G	N	N	N	N	N
G	N	N	N	N	N

Table 4.17: Stage 2: Return on Capital Employed

1992	1993	1994	1995	1996	1992–96 (ave)
G	G	G	G	G	G
N	G	G	N	N	N
N	N	N	N	N	N
G	G	G	N	G	G
N	G	G	G	G	G
N	N	G	G	N	N
N	N	N	N	G	N

Table 4.18: Stage 2: Return on Equity

1992	1993	1994	1995	1996	1992–96 (ave)
G	G	G	G	N	G
N	G	G	N	N	G
N	N	N	N	N	N
G	G	G	G	N	G
N	G	G	G	G	G
N	N	N	N	N	N
N	N	N	N	G	N

◼ Average results of the **green** companies are significantly better than those of their **non-green** rivals in this year
▨ Average results of the **green** companies are better than the **non-green** companies, but the data fails a statistical test
☐ Average results of the **non-green** companies are better than the results of the **green** companies

The data for the support services sector clearly suggest that the green companies out-perform the non-green companies for both of the financial indicators investigated at Stage 1 (Tables 4.15 and 4.16). The data appear inconclusive for the second stage (Tables 4.17 and 4.18).

The strong results for the first stage of the study are supported by a JERU waste management sector survey conducted in 1995 and would suggest that for companies like Shanks & McEwan Group Plc and Waste Recycling Group, which are included in the support services analysis, a progressive environmental approach has a real impact on the profitability of such companies.

The idea that waste management companies could benefit from a reduction in waste is on the face of it contradictory, however many waste management companies more than compensate for decreasing volumes of waste through the provision of waste management consulting services, and in other ways such as renewable energy generation and the sale of recycled materials. Shanks & McEwan derive 5 per cent of annual income from recycling, they encourage pre-sorting of waste particularly if this is commercially valid, and they have reduced compliance costs from a peak of £49,500 in 1992 to £0 in 1995. WRG derives 30 per cent of its revenue through recycling, is undertaking research and development to increase this and uses its landfill gas for sale to grid.

These green companies have been operating on a somewhat uneven playing field however. Many of the larger waste management companies went to considerable expense in improving their landfill operating standards in expectation of landfill licensing which was postponed twice by the Department of the Environment at the last minute. The decision not to insist on higher standards at landfills already in operation gave advantages to the smaller and less conscientious operators. This is one case where a decision to be an environmental step ahead leads to clear competitive disadvantage, although criminal prosecution for mismanagement of landfill sites under the provisions of the Environmental Protection Act 1990 may eventually catch up with many of the 'cowboy' operators.

The lack of positive results may be due to the fact that this is a fairly diverse sector with information technology and human resource firms in the same listing as waste management companies.

Food Retailers

Number of green companies analysed: Five

Table 4.19: Stage 1: Return on Capital Employed

1992	1993	1994	1995	1996	1992–96 (ave)
N	N	N	N	N	N
N	N	N	N	G	N
N	N	N	N	G	N
N	N	N	N	G	N
N	N	N	N	N	N

Table 4.20: Stage 1: Return on Equity

1992	1993	1994	1995	1996	1992–96 (ave)
G	G	G	G	G	G
G	G	N	N	N	N
G	G	G	G	G	G
G	G	G	G	G	G
N	N	N	N	N	N

Table 4.21: Stage 2: Return on Capital Employed

1992	1993	1994	1995	1996	1992–96 (ave)
N	N	N	N	N	N
N	N	N	N	G	N
N	N	N	N	G	N
N	N	N	N	G	N
N	N	N	N	N	N

Table 4.22: Stage 2: Return on Equity

1992	1993	1994	1995	1996	1992–96 (ave)
G	G	G	G	G	G
G	G	N	N	N	N
G	G	G	G	G	G
G	G	G	G	G	G
N	N	N	N	N	N

Average results of the **green** companies are significantly better than those of their **non-green** rivals in this year
Average results of the **green** companies are better than the **non-green** companies, but the data fails a statistical test
Average results of the **non-green** companies are better than the results of the **green** companies

Apart from Table 4.20 which shows the green companies performing better with regard to return on equity at Stage 1 the non-green food retailers do better. This sector was problematic because not only was the green sample size small, but the actual sector is small and difficulty was experienced in identifying enough companies of similar profile for comparison.

One might expect a larger sample to show more positive results. The fierce competition between major food retailers has promoted differentiation not only through the provision of nappy changing facilities and queue minimisation, but in the promotion of green products and reduction and reuse of packaging waste. In the late 1990's food retailers have also begun to take more responsibility for their contribution to packaging waste. This is likely to cost money in the short term without much visible benefit, however companies which solve these issues early are likely to take advantage of low landfill costs, as these costs will almost certainly rise disproportionately in the next few years. Through careful negotiation with waste management companies, supermarkets should be able to alleviate their disposal costs.

Companies are also beginning to be more aware of where they source their products from. Sainsbury's introduced the Integrated Crop Management Scheme (ICMS) in 1991 in response to perceived concern from consumers about pesticide use and residues in food. The Advisory Committee on Business and Environment used this scheme as a case study when they investigated commercial opportunities from environmental initiatives by business. They concluded that although ICMS had a positive impact on the company in terms of ensuring the quality of their food supply and generating marketing and public relations benefit for the company, the impact of such 'intangibles' on sales and profits was difficult to identify. However the case study suggested that Sainsburys acted on the commercial imperative to safeguard its food supplies and maintain their reputation, something which in a sector so highly visible to the public is an important consideration.

Paper, Packaging & Printing

Number of green companies analysed: Four

Table 4.23: Stage 1: Return on Capital Employed

1992	1993	1994	1995	1996	1992–96 (ave)
G	N	N	N	G	N
G	N	G	G	G	G
N	G	G	G	G	G
G	N	N	N	N	N

Table 4.24: Stage 1: Return on Equity

1992	1993	1994	1995	1996	1992–96 (ave)
N	N	N	N	N	N
G	N	G	G	G	G
N	G	G	G	G	G
G	N	N	N	N	N

Table 4.25: Stage 2: Return on Capital Employed

1992	1993	1994	1995	1996	1992–96 (ave)
B	B	B	B	B	B
G	B	G	G	G	G
B	G	G	G	B	B
G	B	B	B	B	B

Table 4.26: Stage 2: Return on Equity

1992	1993	1994	1995	1996	1992–96 (ave)
B	B	B	B	B	B
G	B	B	G	G	G
B	G	G	G	G	G
B	B	B	B	B	B

Average results of the **green** companies are significantly better than those of their **non-green** rivals in this year

Average results of the **green** companies are better than the **non-green** companies, but the data fails a statistical test

Average results of the **non-green** companies are better than the results of the **green** companies

Intuitively one might pick the financial results of paper, packaging and printing companies as being particularly sensitive to the environmental stance of the company. This is not borne out by the above results. The results show the non-green companies performing significantly better at both stages of analysis. The weight of legislation in this area may in fact confer disadvantages to those companies seeking to achieve policies of strict compliance. If this is the case one would expect these companies to reap 'first mover' advantages once legislation is fully in place, assuming such legislation was actively enforced.

All three of the subsectors analysed above have significant environmental impacts associated with them. The paper industry is increasingly affected by the production and demand for recycled paper. Innovation in this industry has ensured a rise in the quality of recycled and part-recycled papers. A reduction in the use of chlorine in pulp bleaching has also had major implications for the production processes of many paper companies, as has the issue of sustainable forestry management. The printing industry is making progress in the reduction of organic solvents and associated VOC emissions. The 1994 EC Directive on 'Packaging and Packaging Waste' has led to protracted consultation about the responsibility for recovery of waste between V-WRAG, the packaging industry's representative body, and the Department of the Environment. Packaging consumes 2 per cent of annual global crude oil production, and plastic packaging alone accounts for 7 per cent of all the material sent to landfill each year.

Packaging companies on the JERU Approved list include Low & Bonar and British Polythene Industries. Both of these companies undertake programmes in energy and raw material reduction and are proactive in recycling attempts, with BPI recycling or reprocessing 90 Ktonnes of the 250 Ktonnes of polythene it produces. However, the JERU environmental survey of the packaging industry illuminates some of the complications faced by companies in assessing and reducing their environmental impacts. While BPI seeks continuous improvements in the impacts of its raw material use, it notes that this does not always equate to raw material minimisation, since thinner materials use more energy/unit of production. Like Ciba Geigy examining its pigment production technology (Chapter 2), BPI evidently has an environmental information system capable of choosing a solution for reduction of raw material use, which is both beneficial to the environment and has a positive return on investment. Low & Bonar have constraints in terms of recycled material use, as many of its products are used for food packaging. They have however increased their use of single materials aiding recycling efforts further down the chain and thus increasing the attractiveness of their products to consumers.

General Retailers

Number of green companies analysed: Six

Table 4.27: Stage 1: Return on Capital Employed

1992	1993	1994	1995	1996	1992–96 (ave)
G	G	G	G	G	G
N	N	N	N	N	N
G	G	G	N	N	N
G	G	G	N	N	G
G	G	G	G	G	G
N	N	N	N	N	N

Table 4.28: Stage 1: Return on Equity

1992	1993	1994	1995	1996	1992–96 (ave)
G	G	G	G	N	G
N	N	N	N	N	N
N	N	N	N	N	N
G	G	G	N	G	G
G	G	G	G	G	G
G	G	N	N	N	G

Table 4.29: Stage 2: Return on Capital Employed

1992	1993	1994	1995	1996	1992–96 (ave)
G	G	G	G	G	G
N	N	G	G	N	N
G	N	G	N	N	N
N	N	N	N	N	N
N	N	N	N	N	N
N	N	N	N	N	N

Table 4.30: Stage 2: Return on Equity

1992	1993	1994	1995	1996	1992–96 (ave)
G	G	G	G	N	N
N	N	G	N	N	N
N	N	N	N	N	N
N	N	N	N	N	N
N	N	N	N	N	N
G	G	N	N	N	G

Overall the results at Stages 1 and 2 suggest the green firms to be profiting from their environmental policies although 1995 and 1996 appear to have been bad years for them relative to their non-green rivals.

A survey in 1996 conducted by JERU revealed that few companies are pursuing environmental improvement in this sector and some retail companies do not even think the environmental debate to be of relevance to their operations This is clearly not the case as retail companies are in an ideal position to encourage the rise of the green consumer and the promotion of environmentally preferable products through supplier assessment. Retailers also have significant impacts on energy use, water consumption, emissions through distribution of goods and land-take through building programmes and out-of-town shopping centres.

Marks and Spencer plc, one of the companies on the Approved list, are an oft-lauded example of good general management practice and it is perhaps not surprising that this extends to a company environmental management system. The retail sector is particularly competitive and in the public eye, and as such is an ideal arena for the recognition of the value added by sound environmental practice. Marks and Spencer undertake energy and packaging efficiency efforts and set quantified targets in these areas. Over 75 per cent of their foods and increasing amounts of their clothes are transported in returnable containers which leads to significant distribution cost savings.

Building Materials & Merchants

Number of green companies analysed: Five

Table 4.31: Stage 1: Return on Capital Employed

1992	1993	1994	1995	1996	1992–96 (ave)
G	G	G	G	G	G
G	G	G	N	N	G
N	N	N	N	N	N
G	G	G	G	G	G
G	G	G	G	G	G

Table 4.32: Stage 1: Return on Equity

1992	1993	1994	1995	1996	1992–96 ave)
G	G	G	G	G	G
G	G	G	N	N	G
G	N	N	N	N	N
G	G	G	G	G	G
G	G	G	G	G	G

Table 4.33: Stage 2: Return on Capital Employed

1992	1993	1994	1995	1996	1992–96 (ave)
G	G	G	G	G	G
N	N	G	N	N	N
N	N	N	N	N	N
G	G	G	G	N	G
G	G	G	G	G	G

Table 4.34: Stage 2: Return on Equity

1992	1993	1994	1995	1996	1992–96(ave)
G	G	G	G	G	G
G	G	G	N	N	G
N	N	N	N	N	N
G	G	N	N	N	N
G	G	G	G	G	G

Green companies perform well relative to non-green companies in all years investigated in the building sector. In only one year at Stage 2 (Table 4.33), did the non-green companies on average perform better.

One of the innovative approaches being taken by the companies in this sector is the use of travelling thermocouples by Baggeridge Brick, one of the firms analysed here, and a Jupiter approved list company. Baggeridge teamed up with the University of Keele and British Ceramic Research to investigate how energy efficiency could be improved in their brick manufacture plant through the use of travelling thermocouples linked to a data acquisition unit in the tunnel kiln. They discovered that by analysing the data collected they could more accurately set the temperature for firing, reducing the amount of energy used and minimising surface staining on the bricks caused by carbon burn out. The throughput of the kiln increased by 40 per cent and the specific energy requirement dropped by 11 per cent. An initial investment of £13,100, had a pay back period of three months, and they recoup £56,000 annually from improved kiln firing efficiency and faster production.

Figure 4.1: Stage 1: All Companies

31%

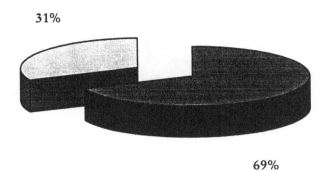

69%

Figure 4.2: Stage 2: All Companies

54%

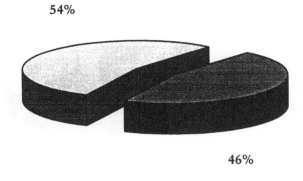

46%

Figure 4.3: Stage 1: Electrical and Electronic Equipment

17%

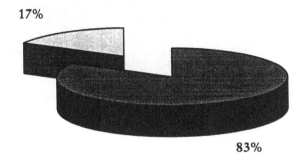

83%

Figure 4.4: Stage 2: Electrical and Electronic Equipment

46%

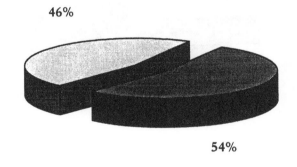

54%

Figure 4.5: Stage 1: Engineering

19%

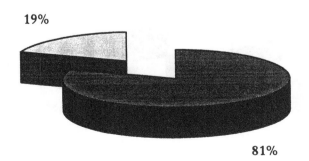

81%

Figure 4.6: Stage 2: Engineering

42%

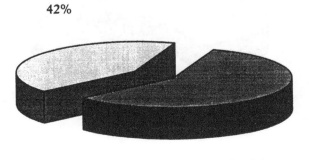

58%

▓ green companies

☐ non-green companies

Figure 4.7: Stage 1: Healthcare

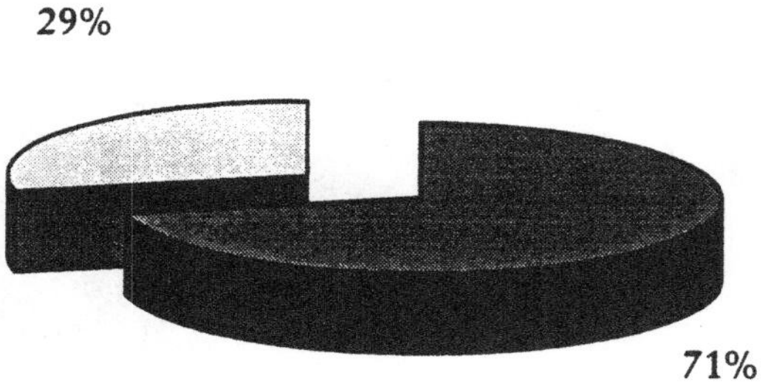

29%

71%

Figure 4.8: Stage 2: Healthcare

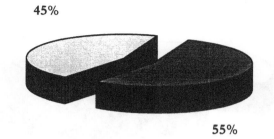

45%

55%

Figure 4.9: Stage 1: Support Services

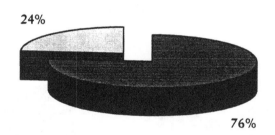

24%

76%

Figure 4.10: Stage 2: Support Services

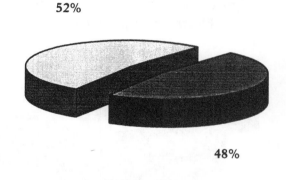

52%

48%

Figure 4.11: Stage 1: Food Retailers

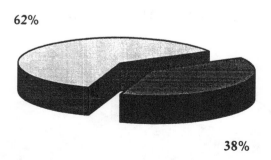

62%

38%

Figure 4.12: Stage 2: Food Retailers

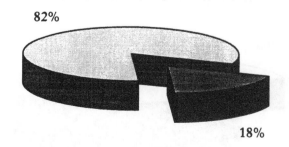

82%

18%

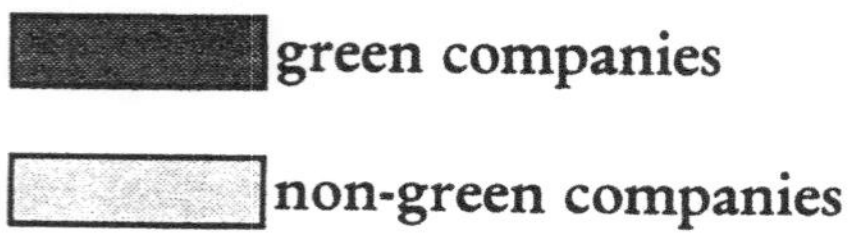

green companies

non-green companies

Figure 4.13: Stage 1: Paper, Packaging and Printing

50%

50%

Figure 4.14: Stage 2: Paper, Packaging and Printing

62%

38%

Figure 4.15: Stage 1: General Retailers

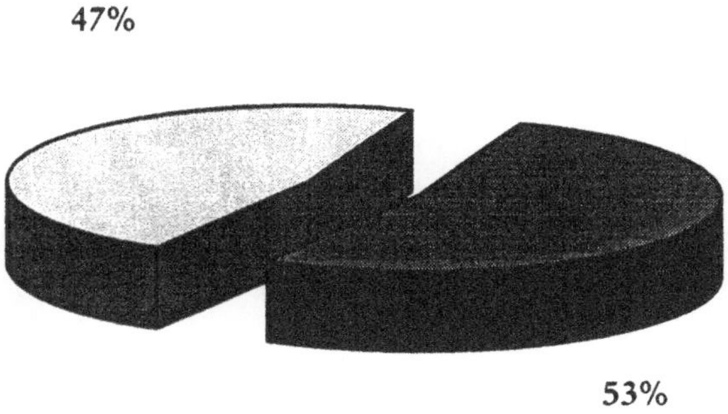

47%

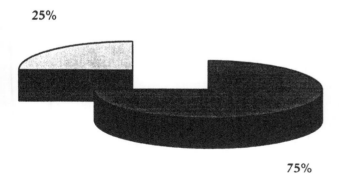

53%

Figure 4.16: Stage 2: General Retailers

75%

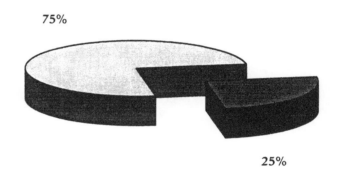

25%

Figure 4.17: Stage 1: Building Materials and Merchants

25%

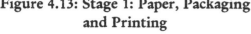

75%

Figure 4.18: Stage 2: Building Materials and Merchants

40%

60%

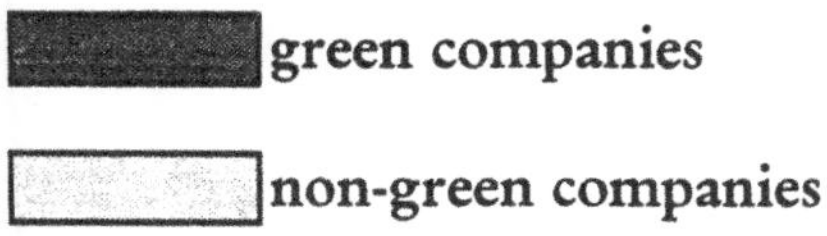

■ green companies

□ non-green companies

Summary

It can be concluded from the data presented that a positive link between environmental and financial performance has been strongly suggested for most of the sectors analysed.

Figs 4.1 and 4.2 show the results of 1,200 direct comparisons between green and non-green companies. In over two thirds of the comparisons at Stage 1, the green companies perform better. Even at Stage 2 where the best financial performers from the non-green sample have been selected for comparison, the green companies perform almost as well. Environmental excellence appears to be rewarded in the bottom-line financial health of many companies. At the second, more rigorous stage of the study where hand-picked financial 'stars' are compared with the green companies, the results are not as conclusive, but a positive correlation is still suggested.

CHAPTER 5
DISCUSSION

A Synergy of Green Motivators

There are good reasons for a possible link between environmental performance and healthy profits. Schmidheimy and Zorraquin (1995), believe that the power of the effect does not reside with any one green issue or business attitude, but in their synergy. Many of the motivators for increased eco-efficiency which they list in their recent book 'Financing Change'(with the World Business Council on Sustainable Development), are growing in importance both in financial terms and because of the growing awareness of the general public. They assert that, in many parts of the world:

- regulations are getting tougher and, more importantly, enforcement is getting tougher;
- more use is being made of economic instruments to encourage constant improvement;
- banks are more willing to lend to cleaner companies;
- insurers are more willing to insure cleaner companies;
- investors are increasingly interested in investing in cleaner companies;
- the best and the brightest are more willing to work for cleaner companies;
- 'green consumerism' is maturing, with the general public believing it has a growing right to have a say in what companies do;
- the search for eco-efficiency can motivate a company and its employees to become more innovative on many fronts;
- eco-efficiency is an excellent avenue for introducing the concept of total quality management;
- media coverage of pollution and environmental liability problems is becoming more sophisticated; and
- many relatives of company directors are becoming more concerned and sophisticated about environment and social issues.

[Schmidheimy and Zorraquin 1995]

Schmidheimy and Zorraquin suggest that: 'Individually, any single one of the reasons listed here for companies to become more eco-efficient might be dismissed as unconvincing. The power lies in the summation of the parts' (1995).

The anecdotal evidence to suggest that companies can profit from the environment is strong; however, this must be tempered by the realisation that no firm wishes to publicise bad news. It is likely that environmental investments with negative payback are far more common than the literature suggests. Not even the most transparent and enlightened company likes to wash its dirty laundry in public. However, companies should not be shy of making public their successes in coping with their individual environmental challenges. A report from ICF Kaiser suggests that a key component of a successful environmental management system is the ability to achieve successful strategic environmental communication. This study looked at the effect of sound environmental company policy on the 'Beta' (a measure of a given stock's volatility relative to the overall market) of 300 US firms. They conclude:

> *Environmental improvements such as those we have evaluated might lead to a substantial reduction in the perceived risk of a firm, with an accompanying increase in a public company's stock price, of perhaps five percent.*
>
> [ICF Kaiser 1997]

The use of the word 'perceived' is instructive. The market cannot know in which direction a firm's intentions lie unless the firm communicates effectively. ICF Kaiser outline a range of methods for communicating environmental management activities and performance to the capital markets, including press releases, environmental reports, (stand-alone or incorporated into the main company report), television commercials, newspaper advertisements and participation in industry initiatives.

The environmental climate is dynamic and ever-changing and environmental investments are subject to a whole range of factors in constant flux. These include regulatory emphasis, economic instruments, consumer behaviour, the culture of the company and the financial position of the company at the time the green investment is being considered. These tensions differ little from those analysed in traditional investment appraisal; however, the information needed to evaluate them is often unrecognised or of poor quality. Companies such as Ciba Geigy which have environmental information systems capable of gathering quantified and costed emissions data on individual products and processes, are equipped to quickly take advantage of changes in any one of the elements of green cost-benefit analysis.

Proactive vs Reactive Cultures

Piesse neatly categorises firms as being proactive environmental spenders or reactive environmental spenders. Proactively spending companies anticipate legislation and voluntarily spend more than the regulator requires. The environmental expenditure of reactive companies is generally in the form of fines or clean-up expenses imposed following violations.

When a proactive spender undertakes environmental expenditure ahead of legislation, there may be reduced earnings, lower dividends and the possibility of the market and other stakeholders judging the expense as unnecessary. However, if the company has judged future legislation correctly it will have benefited from the fact that it has made such expenditure at a convenient time rather than being forced to interrupt operations when forced by legislation to do so. Piesse also mentions that such expenditure may be made a lower cost of capital, expenditure on green technology may be depreciated over the life of an asset rather than incurring a fine which is a one period loss, and such expenditures may act as a tax shield, thus having less effect on dividends than a fine which is not tax deductible.

Retroactive spending such as fines, law suits and clean-up costs can be considerable. Cleaning contaminated land or polluted groundwater may require substantial sums simply to comply with regulatory standards. This will negatively and randomly affect cash flows. Such costs directly impact the profit and loss account of the year in which they occur, they are not anticipated and are likely to affect both earnings and dividends and therefore share price. In addition to such quantifiable effects, market sentiment may also work against such companies, although shareholder behaviour is difficult to unravel in practice.

It appears that forward-thinking companies which engage in anticipatory expenditure in the spirit of the precautionary principle emphasised by both the European Commission and the United Nations Rio and Kyoto summits, are not unduly penalised by the markets for doing so, but that companies which drag their 'eco-footprint' may expect to suffer disproportionately negative market reactions.

Future Research

The direction of causation of a link between being green and profitable has not been addressed by this report. This analysis would require the use of comparable environmental time-series data which is currently unavailable in the UK.

The direction of future research in this area should concentrate on the quality of the environmental information that is gathered. The environmental data used for this report are the best available but they are weak in terms of quantification and thus comparability between companies.

Future investigations using similar data should look at industry effects on the relationship between environmental and financial performance. Is the relationship more pronounced in dirty industries than clean industries? Poole and Mansley's 1996 study would suggest not, although their data set was small. This effect should be investigated in a more systematic and comprehensive way. One might expect that in the chemicals industry, where environmental expenditure has risen to around 20 per cent of corporate capital expenditure, that an environmental investment decision would have more impact on the company financial position and relative competitive position than companies in low pollution industries like healthcare. Companies in low pollution sectors may enjoy a less stringent regulatory environment and the costs and benefits may be less pronounced. Of course this may cause impact in both directions as a company in the chemicals sector will benefit more than a healthcare company from failure to invest in emissions reduction technology in anticipation of legislation that does not materialise.

Future Trends and Influences

The early 1990s have seen much new environmental regulation such as the Environment Act 1990, the Water Resources Act 1991 and the Environment Act 1995, which includes the formation of the new Environment Agency. This agency combines the functions of the Waste Regulation Authorities, Her Majesty's Inspectorate of Pollution and the National Rivers Authority. While it is likely that the pace of new environmental legislation will slow, the effects of the implementation of both the Environment Act and new European legislation like the draft directive on Integrated Pollution Prevention and Control, will be increasingly felt by industry. Many of the key Environment Agency personnel including the new chairman Ed Gallagher were recruited from the NRA, and if they pursue as vigorous an enforcement policy as the NRA, business can expect to be closely monitored and held to account for environmental misdemeanours.

The influence of information technology will increasingly affect the environmental management of companies. More use is likely to be made of the Internet both as an information source for companies who are planning environmental strategies, and as a communication tool for enhanced stakeholder relations. Companies are beginning to develop software to complement environmental management systems, like the British Airways 'Environmental Toolkit' – an internal environmental audit tool. Such uses of information technology is likely to aid the process of identifying and responding to environmental problems and opportunities.

As suggested earlier, companies with mature and sophisticated environmental policies may find financially positive environmental investment increasingly difficult to identify as all of the possibilities for resource efficiency are exhausted. However, the small number of companies that produce an environmental report might suggest that there are few companies seriously engaging in environmental performance improvement and that the problem of diminishing returns is a distant one. The onus to sustain the momentum of environmental efforts that financially reward companies, lies partly with the companies themselves through the use of innovative and creative technology and partly with the regulators. They must support industrial efforts through the use of flexible and well-constructed legislation, written in consultation with key industry players, and with economic instruments, such as subsidies or pollution charges, that work with, rather than against, market forces.

Elkington (1996) suggests the company of the future will be forced, by a drive towards more sustainable economic growth, to take account of and add value to a triple bottom line of economic, ethical and environmental considerations. Businesses are constantly adapting to challenges that result from changes in the business environment, such as the quickening global economy, advances in technology and demographic change.

Bruce Smart, a Senior Fellow at the World Resources Institute commented:

> *A new unsettling variable such as the environment is not unprecedented. Imagine the consternation of nineteenth-century industrialists faced with child labour laws or the dismay of their successors contemplating the new income tax. These dramatically altered their costs and changed their business practices. In such circumstances, farsighted and nimble companies prosper and laggards decline. Such is the way of a dynamic economic system.*

[Smart 1994]

Businesses should be capable of the development of management systems and frameworks, to confront and profit from the challenge that achieving environmental excellence presents.

CHAPTER 6
CONCLUSIONS

The purpose of this study was to examine the relationship between environmental and financial performance of companies. The following conclusions and recommendations emerge:

- The hypothesis that good environmental performance leads to better financial results than bad environmental performance is strongly supported by the data presented. It appears that most good environmental performers do not pay a penalty for their efforts.

- The interaction between the environmental performance of a company, and the revenue and cost structure of the company, is a complex and dynamic one, subject to constantly changing internal and external opportunities and constraints.

- The internal and external constraints and opportunities that are encountered by a company will increasingly reflect the need expressed at the United Nation Conference on Environment and Development in 1992, to move towards more sustainable economic development.

- Companies with environmental information systems capable of gathering data on product- and process-specific environmental impacts, and the costs associated with these, are more likely to be able to make financially positive environmental investment decisions than those without.

- These companies will benefit financially, relative to their competitors, from the ability to take early advantage of changes in the business climate which are highlighted by an environmental information system. Companies are thus advised to develop environmental information systems both to enhance profitability and contribute to industry's role in sustainable development.

APPENDIX A

JUPITER ENVIRONMENTAL RESEARCH UNIT
ASSESSMENT PROCESS

THE ASSESSMENT PROCESS
FOR
GREEN INVESTMENT

A guide to Jupiter Asset Management's approach to assessing companies for green investment funds

Fourth Edition : 1997

Jupiter Environmental Research Unit
Jupiter Asset Management Limited
Regulated by IMRO

Jupiter's Assessment Process : A Summary

Jupiter Asset Management's Green Funds seek to invest in companies that are responding positively to the challenge of environmental sustainability and are making a commitment to social well-being.

Companies in our Green Funds either provide products or services which contribute to social and environmental improvements or act in a way that reduces the adverse external impacts of their operations, or both. Examples of beneficial products or services include:

- environmental technologies and services;
- healthcare products and services;
- public transport;
- telecommunication and information technologies.

Examples of beneficial practices include:

- adherence to health, safety and environmental policy standards;
- management of operations to ensure minimal environmental impact;
- publication of social and environment performance reports;
- world wide implementation of codes of conduct for labour standards.

The Green Funds also seek to avoid investments in industrial activities which are believed to be incompatible with environmental and social goals. Examples of such activities include:

- manufacturing of armaments, alcoholic drinks or tobacco products;
- publication of pornographic material;
- generation of nuclear power;
- operation of gambling facilities.

Accordingly any company which derives over 10 per cent of its turnover from any one of these activities will not be invested in. A company which derives less than 10 per cent of turnover from any one of these activities may be invested in, but only if we believe that it makes an outstanding contribution to sustainable development in other respects.

Additionally the Green Funds will not invest in any company which conducts or commissions animal tests carried out for cosmetic and toiletry purposes. A company involved in animal testing on other products, and their ingredients, will only be suitable for investment if we believe it has made a substantial commitment to minimise animal testing, and in other respects makes an outstanding contribution to sustainable development.

Finally, in order to respond to stock market opportunities, up to 5 per cent of the Green Funds' assets may be invested in companies which appear suitable but for which research is still in progress. If the research into any such company has not been completed within three months of the investment date, the holding will be sold.

Box A.1: Our Philosophy : Emphasising the Positive

The companies that best suit our Green Funds are those which are committed to continuously improving their environmental and social performances. It is therefore the positive actions that companies take to achieve these improvements which are the best indicators of their suitability for our Green Funds. Consequently our research process is primarily based upon assessing positive actions.

Nonetheless we also negatively screen, or filter-out, companies active in those industries which are incompatible with the social and environmental objectives of the Green Funds. However if a company only derives a small proportion of its turnover from one of these proscribed industries but makes an outstanding contribution to sustainable development in some other way, then we may judge that the company is, on balance, suitable for the Green Funds.

An industrial sector where such choices frequently occur is water treatment. Here a number of otherwise excellent companies (in terms of sustainable development) sell small amounts of ultrapure water to nuclear power plants for use in steam boilers. Under conventional negative screening these companies could be barred from ethical funds. However we believe that such companies' positive contributions to sustainable development – by improving aquatic environments and raising the efficiency of water use – are more important, and therefore these companies are suitable for our Green Funds.

We believe that the effects of our investments can also be positive. By investing, the Green Funds can, and do, influence and encourage positive changes in the way that companies are managed. Similarly, we believe that companies' efforts should be recognised – and one way that we can do this is by investing in them.

We think that we can only operate this rational and positive approach to company assessment because we have an in-house research capacity supported by an expert advisory committee. We also believe that this approach not only benefits Jupiter's Green Funds but also the wider sustainable development process.

Jupiter Asset Management and Green Investment

Jupiter Asset Management places emphasis on developing a high-quality business in tune with contemporary needs and, with over £100m of Green Funds under management, is seen as a market leader in the growing sector of green investment. The group's two principal financial products in this area are the Jupiter International Green Investment Trust PLC, which was the first green investment trust to be launched in Europe, and the Jupiter Ecology Fund, which is managed by Jupiter Unit Trust Managers and was the first authorised green unit trust to be launched in the UK. In addition, Jupiter Asset Management manages Green Funds for private clients and charities as well as ethically and environmentally screened pensions and life products for a number of life companies.

The Green Department

Green investment at Jupiter Asset Management is undertaken by the specialist Green Department. The department consists of a Fund Manager, the Jupiter Environmental Research Unit and the Jupiter Environmental Advisory Committee.

The relationship between the three determines the Department's 'twin track' approach to green investment. Companies' financial and ethical/environmental performances are assessed separately. As is shown in the diagram below, only when both performances have been approved may the Green Funds invest.

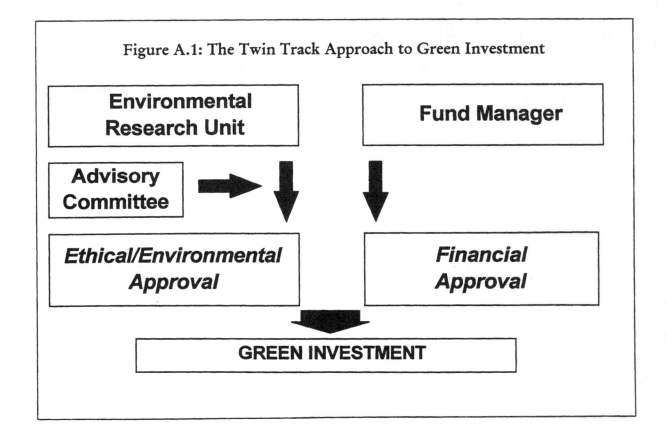

Figure A.1: The Twin Track Approach to Green Investment

The Fund Manager

The Fund Manager, who is head of the Green Department, is responsible for assessing the financial strengths of companies, and for the size and diversity of investments within the portfolios managed by the Green Department. However, he cannot make an investment until approval has been given by the Jupiter Environmental Research Unit.

Simon Baker – *joined Jupiter in August 1994*

Has spent over 20 years in the investment business. Formerly managed the Charities Official Investment Fund. Also was head of UK equities at MGM.

The Jupiter Environmental Research Unit (JERU)

There are three members of JERU, a team of environmental and social scientists which analyses the ethical and environmental performances of companies. JERU's main objective is to create an Approved List of companies that demonstrate good practice regarding ethical and environmental issues.

Emma Howard Boyd – *joined Jupiter in September 1994*

Formerly a corporate finance executive with Hill Samuel and Banque National de Paris. Also worked for Women's Environmental Network and the Social Investment Forum.

Charles Millar – *joined Jupiter in November 1994*

Has an MSc in Environmental Technology. Formerly an environmental consultant who has also worked for a range of environmental Non Governmental Organisations.

Michael Tyrrell – *joined Jupiter in November 1996*

Has an MSc in Environmental Technology. Formerly worked for an environmental consultancy and an environmental charity.

The Jupiter Environmental Advisory Committee

The Jupiter Environmental Advisory Committee is a team of eminent environmentalists who advise JERU on company research. The Committee meets quarterly, but members are consulted frequently between meetings. Their advice focuses on the following issues:

- criteria for assessing companies' performances;
- current environmental trends;
- questions of business ethics.

The members of the Jupiter Environmental Advisory Committee are profiled below.

David Astor – Chairman

Director of the Jupiter International Green Investment Trust PLC. Past Chairman of the Council for the Protection of Rural England.

Sir Martin Holdgate

Environmental scientist. President of the Zoological Society of London, member of The Royal Commission on Environmental Pollution. Past Director General of IUCN – The World Conservation Union.

Stanley Johnson

Environmentalist and author. Past Head of Prevention of Pollution and Nuisances Division, EEC. 1984 Greenpeace Award for Outstanding Services to Conservation.

Our Assessment Criteria

The negative criteria

In making a balanced judgement of a company we need to identify its shortcomings as well as its merits. Our negative criteria concern involvement in industrial activities that we believe are incompatible with environmental and social improvement.

If a company derives more than 10 per cent of its turnover from any one of these businesses it will not be invested in. However if a company derives less than 10 per cent of its turnover from any one of these businesses, but we believe that in other respects it makes an outstanding contribution to sustainable development, then the Green Funds may invest.

Alcoholic drinks
Alcoholic drink can, in moderation, be beneficial to health. However it is widely held that alcohol abuse can be the cause of a wide variety of problems ranging from ill health and domestic violence to road accidents. There is also concern about the impact of recently developed "alcopops" amongst younger drinkers. In view of these concerns, any company which derives in excess of 10 per cent of turnover from the manufacture or sale of alcoholic drinks will not be added to the Approved List.

Animal testing
JERU believes that there is no justification for continuing to commission or conduct animal tests for cosmetic and toiletry purposes. Accordingly any company which commissions or conducts such tests will be barred from the Approved List.

The Green Funds will also not invest in retail companies which commission or conduct animal tests on "own label" cosmetic and toiletry products or their ingredients. For all other products the Green Funds operate a positive screening approach which seeks evidence of companies' commitment to alternatives to animal testing. This is set out on page 11 of this document.

Armaments
The armaments business involves the manufacture and trade of goods and services specifically designed for military purposes. This includes the component parts of armaments. Although armaments may be used for self defence or peacekeeping purposes, it is frequently difficult to determine their final use. Accordingly companies deriving more than 10 per cent of their turnover from the armaments business are barred from the Approved List.

JERU distinguishes armaments manufacturers from the broader *defence contracting* business which includes companies that provide civilian goods – such as paint or office equipment – to defence related customers. We believe that companies which provide civilian goods to these customers should not be excluded from the Green Funds.

Gambling

The potentially addictive nature of gambling and its consequent impact upon individuals and families, and especially those in lower income groups, has long been a cause of concern. Accordingly any company which derives in excess of 10 per cent of its turnover from gambling will not be included on the Approved List.

In addition to companies such as book-makers and casino operators this criterion may affect retailers selling lottery tickets and scratch cards, as well as corporate members of the UK's National Lottery consortium.

Nuclear power

In comparison to fossil-fuel fired power stations, nuclear power stations produce minimal amounts of greenhouse gases and many other airborne emissions. However the risks arising from accidental discharges of radioactive substances from nuclear power stations and the lack of acceptable disposal facilities for high level and intermediate radioactive waste are held by many people to be reason enough to regard this industry as unacceptable.

This argument provides the basis for Jupiter's Green Funds' avoidance of companies which build nuclear power stations, or those which generate nuclear powered electricity. Accordingly any company which derives in excess of 10 per cent of its turnover from these activities will fail to pass this negative screen and will not be added to the Approved List.

Pornography

Pornography has been linked to the continued problem of sexual discrimination as well as to more obvious concerns over its corrupting influence on behaviour. This is why Jupiter's Green Funds avoid companies involved in pornography.

With recent advances in communications technology and the rapid evolution of the media sector the criterion is now relevant to companies which supply or distribute pornographic material electronically as well as to more established businesses such as retailers and publishers of pornographic magazines. Accordingly any company which derives in excess of 10 per cent of its turnover from the publication or distribution of pornographic material will fail to pass this negative screen and will not be added to the Approved List.

Tobacco

That tobacco products are responsible for very substantial health problems now appears to be acknowledged by the manufacturers themselves. As this health message has led to a decline in the number of smokers in Western countries, so the tobacco majors have expanded their marketing efforts in developing economies.

Both the evidence of health effects and objections to the marketing practices in developing countries make the tobacco industry a business sector which many investors wish to avoid. Accordingly any company which derives in excess of 10 per cent of turnover from the manufacture of tobacco products will fail to pass a negative screen and will not be added to the Approved List.

Exceptions to the negative criteria

'Must take' contracts
In a few cases, companies are legally obliged to do business with industries which breach our negative criteria. In such circumstances we exempt them from our normal negative screening process. For example, as over 20 per cent of the UK's electricity is generated at nuclear power stations, companies involved in supplying electricity are significantly dependent upon nuclear power. As these companies have no option but to purchase nuclear power – under so called 'must take' contracts – we feel it would be inappropriate to bar them from our Approved List.

Investment funds
In exceptional circumstances our Green Funds may make investments in other investment funds which have stated environmental or ethical objectives. The purpose of these investments is to give our Green Funds exposure to investment opportunities which may not otherwise be accessible. As all ethical funds have slightly different negative criteria, these funds may not always wholly meet the criteria of our own Green Funds. In such circumstances JERU will consider the relative merits of the investment and make a balanced judgement upon its suitability for the Green Funds.

Industries subject to special scrutiny

Jupiter's Green Funds currently avoid investments in certain businesses which we believe have disproportionately large adverse impacts upon the environment or society. Due to their particular effects these are subject to special scrutiny by JERU. Some of the key sectors in this category are listed below.

Banking and financial services
Although many banks and financial services companies publicly endorse the concept of sustainable development, Jupiter's Green Funds have generally avoided the sector because of the difficulty of determining whether their operations assist other companies to breach the Green Fund's other ethical and environmental criteria.

The Green Funds will only invest in companies which demonstrate systematic ethical and environmental screening processes for corporate loans and asset management operations. Additionally, banks which have a particularly small proportion of their loans going to commercial borrowers may be suitable for investment, subject to their passing JERU's other screens.

Bio-technology
In many instances bio-technology is simply a more precise and predictable way of achieving the same ends as selective breeding. In such cases, involving the combination of genetic material from individuals of the same or closely related species, the process can produce substantial improvements to crop plants or other economically valuable species whilst incurring only minimal risk of environmental harm.

However some other combinations – such as those designed to increase the virulence of viruses that may be used in pest control – cause concern because of the risks they might cause in the environment. There may also be important implications for animal welfare arising from some of the technologies. As the risks and benefits are often difficult to assess in this sector, which is one of rapid innovation, Jupiter's Green Funds will only invest in bio-technology companies after extensive discussions with the Advisory Committee.

Poly Vinyl Chloride
There is widespread concern over the manufacture and use of PVC. Some emissions from PVC manufacturing may be carcinogenic and have also been linked to birth deformities in humans and animals. Accordingly JERU believes that there is a case for phasing-out the use of PVC. However, as the PVC manufacturing industry is substantial and the product is very widely used, such a phase-out cannot be achieved immediately. Hence, the Green Funds favour companies which are seeking alternatives to PVC and are restricting their suppliers to those which operate best production practices.

The Green Funds distinguish between short-life and long-life applications for PVC. Short life applications are essentially packaging-related and are particularly inappropriate given the toxic emissions which can be produced during the disposal of PVC – especially by fire. Companies which manufacture longer life products, such as window frames will be looked upon more favourably, particularly where they identify all their PVC products with the appropriate label.

Transport
Over-dependence upon cars is leading to declining air quality, the loss of open spaces to new road construction and the decline of local town centres. Therefore Jupiter's Green Funds seek to avoid companies which are substantially involved in the manufacture or sale of cars.

The exceptions to this criterion are manufacturers of low or zero emission vehicles and vehicle components which promote road safety or environmental improvement.

The Green Funds also currently seek to avoid investments in airlines because of the environmental problems associated with aircraft fuel consumption and emissions.

The positive criteria

The aim of our positive screening is to identify how comprehensively environmental and social considerations are integrated into corporate actions – in respect to both products and services and to production processes. Satisfactory integration typically involves the adoption of a broad range of measures, including structured management systems, clearly demarcated lines of responsibility and the disclosure of impacts and performances.

Our positive criteria are of varying importance, some being better indicators of good performance than others. Clearly, the better a company performs in respect to the criteria the more chance it has of being added to the Approved List. Due to the largely self-regulatory nature of corporate environmental governance, the majority of the criteria are voluntary for companies.

Animal testing
As was noted before, Jupiter's Green Funds seek to avoid investing in companies which commission or conduct animal testing for cosmetic and toiletry purposes. However, animal testing is also carried-out on a vast range of other every-day products and their ingredients. In

respect to these, the Green Funds are committed to the fastest practicable phase-out of animal testing, but recognise that this will not be rapidly achieved, especially where some such testing is required by law.

Accordingly, the Green Funds will only invest in companies which are actively seeking to minimise their involvement in animal testing. This requires companies making a commitment to the "3Rs" of reduction, refinement and replacement of tests. These are explained below.

Box A.2: The Three Rs of Animal Testing: Reduction, Refinement and Replacement

Reductions in the number of tests can be achieved in several ways. For example, publishing test results prevents the need for repetition. Those companies which publish results, despite the risk of losing-out on commercially sensitive information are considered to be operating best practice.

Refinements in testing are all intended to minimise the suffering of test animals – typically this may involve the extended use of anaesthetics and reduced exposure to other stresses prior to testing.

Replacements of tests typically involve the use of non-animal techniques like in-vitro experiments on cell cultures, or computer modelling. Like all alternatives, replacement techniques cannot perfectly substitute for animal tests in all cases.

When assessing a company in respect to animal testing, JERU therefore seeks evidence of practical support for the 3Rs such as a pro-active approach to disclosing information on the number of tests the company has conducted and whether it is a member of any organisation dedicated to the search for non-animal alternatives – such as the Fund for the Replacement of Animals in Medical Experimentation.

Beneficial products and services

Jupiter's Green Funds actively seek to invest in companies that manufacture products or provide services that have an environmental or social benefit. A selection of these is given below.

Environmental technology manufacturers

Companies which produce emissions control equipment (for example water filters and airborne particulate traps), or renewable energy technologies (for example photovoltaic cells) are favoured by the Green Funds.

Environmental services

Environmental consultancies which advise on environmental performance and companies which operate environmental technologies are favoured by the Green Funds.

Healthcare products and services

Healthcare companies provide a range of products and services which meet the requirements of the Green Funds. Products may include equipment for diagnostics, sterilisation and waste handling for use in surgeries, homecare or hospitals. Services may include the provision of homecare and nursing facilities.

Telecommunications and Information Technologies

Telecommunications and IT are business sectors which are favoured by the Green Funds because of their potential roles in addressing transport problems and the consumption of printed matter. Companies which are making a positive contribution to these solutions will be favoured by the Green Funds.

Transport

The Green Funds favour public transport companies such as railway and bus operators because of their contribution to reducing congestion and airborne pollution. The funds will also favour bicycle manufacturers and other companies which contribute to sustainable transport solutions.

Other products

Companies which provide other socially beneficial products such as educational and safety equipment may be favoured by the Green Funds, as may companies which produce the most environmentally preferable model of a given product. Equally, companies which manufacture products from recycled materials may be favoured.

Disclosure

There is a gradual shift by companies towards greater transparency and openness about their activities. This shift is perhaps most noticeable in the publication of annual environmental reports, although social audits are also now published by a few leading companies. There is no particular format for these reports, however, JERU places emphasis on the quantification of the information that is disclosed and the company's annual performance in relation to stated targets.

JERU supports these initiatives and companies demonstrating particular openness will be favoured by the Green Funds.

Employment and labour standards

Pro-active policies regarding equal employment opportunities – addressing issues such as training, childcare facilities, flexible working-hours and wheelchair access – are becoming increasingly common in UK companies. JERU supports such initiatives and favours companies that are taking a lead in this respect, for example through participation in such schemes as the UK's Investors in People.

Overseas, the labour standards to which companies operate are also important. JERU seeks companies that are committed to raising their standards in all operations up to the level of best practice. Increasingly, attention is being paid to the standards operated by suppliers, particularly in businesses like clothing and sports goods manufacturing.

One way of addressing this issue is by adopting and operating to a Code of Practice. These codes, which are being developed by aid agencies such as Oxfam and Christian Aid, take into account a range of activities (see below). JERU actively promotes the adoption of such Codes and favours the companies which are taking a lead in this evolving area – particularly in respect to the monitoring and verification of performance.

```
┌─────────────────────────────────────────────────────────────┐
│              Box A.3: Issues to be Covered by Codes of Practice │
│                                                               │
│   1   Freedom of association and collective bargaining        │
│   2   Equality of treatment                                   │
│   3   Wages                                                   │
│   4   Working hours                                           │
│   5   Health and safety                                       │
│   6   Security of employment                                  │
│   7   Social security                                         │
│   8   Environment                                            │
│   9   Child labour                                           │
│   10  Forced labour                                          │
└─────────────────────────────────────────────────────────────┘
```

Environmental management

Clearly, one of the key factors in determining a company's suitability for inclusion in any green fund is the way it manages its external environmental effects and thereby reduces its negative impact upon the wider environment.

JERU not only seeks to find those companies that already have comprehensive environmental management systems in place but also those companies that are committed to continuously improving their performance by systematically implementing environmentally sound management procedures. Although companies demonstrate their commitment to environmental protection in different ways, key indicators include the following:

Corporate environmental policy

Companies that publish environmental policy statements committing themselves to substantive action, will be favoured by JERU particularly when the policy is effectively communicated to company stakeholders.

Environmental Management Systems

Companies are not obliged to follow any particular model of environmental management system. However an undertaking to apply the International Standards Organisation's Environmental Management System (ISO14001) or the European Community's Eco-management and Audit Scheme (EMAS) is regarded as a good indicator of the structured commitment to environmental management that JERU seeks.

Monitoring environmental impact

The effective operation of an environmental management system depends on how well a company monitors its own environmental performance. Accordingly, JERU seeks companies that are conducting regular environmental audits and encourages third party verification.

Trading partner assessments

JERU believes that corporate responsibility for the environmental impact of products extends from cradle-to-grave or from raw material extraction through to final disposal. Consequently, JERU seeks companies that scrutinise the environmental performance of their suppliers and contractors by means of questionnaires, audits or dialogue. JERU particularly favours companies that use their position as buyers to improve the environmental performance of their trading partners.

Energy efficiency

As one of the simplest potential environmental improvements, energy efficiency initiatives indicate a company's commitment to reduce its environmental impact. In particular, JERU seeks companies that aim to improve their efficiency by continuously setting and meeting ever tightening targets.

Responsibility and communication

JERU prefers companies to operate a formal hierarchy of environmental accountability from board level down and to keep employees fully informed, trained and involved in the environmental effects of their work.

Greenhouse gases

Commercial activities carry a large part of the responsibility for global warming – principally through their direct and indirect emissions of carbon dioxide, although smaller emissions of other, often more potent, greenhouse gases also make a significant contribution. Although the full impact of global warming is far from understood, it is expected to disrupt weather patterns. This will affect natural bio-systems as well as human activity. Whilst some wild species and some societies will be able to adapt, many will be seriously threatened.

The Green Funds recognise these threats and favour companies which minimise emissions of greenhouse gases. In practice the best way that companies can achieve this is by reducing their dependency on fossil fuels. In the many instances where the source of electricity is beyond a company's control, the best way of diminishing its contribution to carbon emissions is therefore by improving energy efficiency.

The Green Funds also seek to invest in companies which produce goods and services that promote energy efficiency or reduce greenhouse gases emissions in other ways – in particular in respect to alternatively powered transport systems and non-fossil fuel electricity generation.

Human rights

Although there is widespread concern over corporate operations in countries with poor human rights records, we believe that companies' should be judged by their own standards rather than by the records of the countries in which they operate. This is because companies can act as a force for good in countries with low standards and they should not be penalised for this. However, companies which have substantial dealings with oppressive regimes or which take advantage of lax labour laws, will not be favoured by JERU.

Legal compliance

We believe that compliance with regulations should be a minimum standard rather than a target for companies, particularly for those in a green portfolio. Accordingly JERU assesses whether companies are, or have been, the subject of prosecution or litigation or have otherwise attracted adverse attention from regulatory bodies.

Companies with a poor compliance history will not be barred from the Approved List if there is clear evidence that systems exist to ensure that the problems are not repeated.

Ozone depleting substances

The depletion of the protective ozone layer in the upper atmosphere is one of the most pressing global environmental problems. Significant contributors to this problem are chlorine and bromine based gases used in refrigeration, fire extinguishing and other industrial processes.

JERU recognises that phasing-out ozone depleting substances can be very complicated as it may involve replacing pumps, piping and much other equipment. However the severity of the problem is such that the phase-out is vital. The Green Funds therefore invest in companies which are moving towards a total cessation of their use of ozone depleting substances and in the interim are actively reducing leakage. Similarly, the Green Funds favour companies involved in the development and sale of non-depleting alternatives, such as hydro-carbon based refrigerants.

Packaging and labelling

By lengthening products' lives, improving transport efficiencies and reducing breakages, packaging products substantially reduce resource wastage. However packaging products also consume sizeable resources themselves and give rise to widespread disposal problems. Companies at all stages in the packaging chain have a shared responsibility for remedying the problem of packaging waste. One way of addressing this waste problem is by labelling packaging products in order to identify their constituent parts and so facilitate their recovery and reuse.

JERU favours companies actively seeking to minimise their packaging waste by reducing, reusing or recycling and labelling packaging products.

Sustainable agriculture

Recent health scares in the food industry, particularly regarding the link between BSE and the new form of CJD in people, have accentuated concerns about the increasing industrialisation of agriculture. The problems associated with the agri-business are, of course, not restricted to the safety of human food supplies. Livestock welfare issues are a major concern, particularly those involving transport, slaughter, living space and the use of growth hormones. To many, the use of fertilisers and pesticides on crops is equally disturbing – because of their environmental impact as well as the possibility of accumulating levels of these substances in the food chain.

JERU recognises these problems and operates stringent policies regarding agricultural produce companies. Only companies which are committed to sustainable agricultural practices, high standards of animal welfare and low chemical input will be added to the Approved List.

Sustainable resource use

There is considerable concern about the unsustainable "mining" of natural resources such as old growth forests and wild fish stocks. The Green Funds favour companies that operate best practice with respect to the sustainable use of these resources through their involvement in "buyers groups" such as the World Wide Fund for Nature's 95+ Group and the Marine Stewardship Council.

In respect to companies whose business involves wild species, JERU favours companies whose actions go beyond compliance in regard to the requirements of the Convention on the International Trade in Endangered Species.

The Green Department's Research Process

The Green Department carries out three basic types of research into companies. These are detailed below.

Preliminary assessment

In order to respond to stock-market opportunities it is sometimes necessary for the Fund Manager to make rapid investment decisions. This may not be possible if a full and detailed assessment of a company's ethical and environmental performance has to be made. Accordingly JERU conducts Preliminary Assessments, which make quick provisional judgements of companies' suitability for inclusion on the Approved List of companies from which the Fund Manager is allowed to invest.

Preliminary Assessments require answers to some basic questions about products and processes. If the answers are satisfactory, the investment will be given Preliminary Approval, which allows it to be held within a portfolio until the Full Assessment is complete. The Full Assessment must be completed within three months of the investment being made.

If the Full Assessment results in the company being approved the investment may be retained. If the company fails the Full Assessment however, it will be given unapproved status and must be divested. As a safeguard to the ethical and environmental integrity of the Green Funds, the amount of companies held with Preliminary Approval will not exceed 5 per cent of the total value of holdings in any portfolio, at the time of the initial investment.

Full assessment

In the overwhelming majority of cases, when there is less urgency to invest, JERU conducts Full Assessments. These use questionnaires from JERU and company publications as a basis for research. Company publications which can be useful include product literature (for details of the content, purpose and potential market of goods and services), annual reports (for listing the location of operations and the presence of potentially controversial subsidiaries), and environmental reports, if they exist, which set out policies and programmes regarding environmental issues. In addition to a standard questionnaire, JERU often develops special questionnaires to address the specific issues affecting individual companies.

In addition and wherever practicable, the Research Unit will visit companies as part of the Full Assessment process. This is because the Research Unit believes that dialogue with company management and other personnel can provide a particularly telling insight into the company's approach to ethical and environmental issues.

If JERU believes the company satisfies the Full Assessment's requirements, it will be added to the Approved List of companies from which the Fund Manager may invest.

Sector assessments

As part of its best in class approach, JERU also conducts Sector Assessments. These aim to identify companies which have the best social and environmental performance within any selected industrial sector.

JERU believes that Sector Assessments are an important aspect of the positive approach to green investment, because within all sectors of industry there is scope for companies to improve their environmental performance and those that are best in class should be recognised and encouraged to continue to improve. Sector leaders will be added to the Approved List provided they do not breach the negative criteria.

Reviewing and removing companies

Review of research
Companies on the Approved List are re-assessed at least once every eighteen months to ensure that they meet the objectives of the Green Funds. Additionally when a significant event, such as a major acquisition, occurs to any company then it may be re-assessed.

Removal from the Approved List
Companies which fail preliminary assessments, and re-assessments, are removed from the Approved List. If a company fails an assessment whilst it is actually held in a portfolio, the Fund Manager is obliged to sell the holding within three months of it being given unapproved status. Removals from the Approved List and disinvestments are reported to the Advisory Committee on a quarterly basis.

Other Activities of the Green Department

Promotion of best practice in environmental and social management

An important element of The Green Department's function is its promotion of improved ethical and environmental performances by companies. JERU use company visits and routine correspondence to raise performance issues with managements. Amongst the actions which JERU most actively promotes are:

- Compliance with voluntary Codes of Conduct regarding employees or suppliers located in developing economies;
- Increases in corporate environmental disclosure regarding both environmental and social performance;
- Integration of environmental issues into mainstream operational management.

Information about the Green Funds

A feature of Jupiter's green investment service is that it keeps its investors informed about their investments. JERU produces two regular publications in addition to the annual and half yearly reports of the Green Funds. These are:

Jupiter Environmental Research Bulletin
The *Bulletin* is published every Spring and Autumn and is sent to all unit holders and other interested parties. It contains the following regular features:

- a list of the entire portfolio of companies invested in by the Jupiter Ecology Fund, with a small profile of each company;
- detailed profiles on a selection of these companies; these profiles may refer to areas of concern as well as to positive developments;
- articles on recent trends and events which may impact upon green investment;
- a guest article from a leading commentator on environmental affairs;
- the financial performance of Jupiter Ecology Fund.

The Jupiter Ecology Fund Fact Sheet

The *Fact Sheet*, which is sent to Independent Financial Advisers and to other enquirers, is published four times each year. It contains the following features:

- details of the short term and long term performance and value of the fund;
- a list of the ten largest holdings in the fund;
- a report on the fund by the investment manager;
- information on The Green Department and on Jupiter Asset Management;
- a summary of the fund's ethical and environmental criteria.

Jupiter's Green Investment Products and Services

The Jupiter Ecology Fund

The Jupiter Ecology Fund, which is an authorised Unit Trust managed by Jupiter Unit Trust Managers, aims to achieve long term capital appreciation together with growing income by investing world-wide in companies that are responding positively to, and profiting from, the challenge of environmental sustainability and have made a positive commitment to social well-being.

- The net asset value of the Ecology Fund at 1 September 1997 was £45.61 million.

- This Ecology Fund is available through the Jupiter PEP.

- PEP Scheme particulars, the Annual and Half-yearly Reports and other information on the Ecology Fund are available from the managers.

The Jupiter International Green Investment Trust Plc

The aim of the Jupiter International Green Investment Trust, which is managed by Jupiter Asset Management, is to provide its shareholders with long term capital appreciation, together with growing income, by investing in companies that are responding positively to the challenge of environmental sustainability and are making a commitment to social well-being.

- The Total Assets of the Trust at 30 June 1997 were £37.025 million.

- The fund is available through a self-select PEP.

- Copies of the Annual Report and Financial Statements and the Interim Report are available from the managers.

Green investment for private and institutional clients

Jupiter Asset Management provides private client and institutional investment management services. Further information on these services is available upon request.

Pension and life products

JAM manages two further green products, on behalf of Lincoln National (UK) PLC and Skandia Life Assurance Company Ltd.

Lincoln Green Fund

The Lincoln Green Fund aims to provide consistent returns by investing in companies that have proven commercial success, but also have clear and effective environmental policies. The Fund is available for a range of Lincoln's life assurance, pension and investment products.

Further information can be obtained from Lincoln on 01452 371 371.

Skandia Ethical Managed Funds

The Skandia Ethical Managed Funds aims to achieve a rate of growth above the average achieved by comparable funds, through a well diversified actively managed portfolio of companies both in the UK and elsewhere, which can clearly demonstrate sound ethical and/or environmental practice. The Skandia Ethical Managed Funds comprise the Skandia Ethical Managed Life and Pension Funds.

Further information can be obtained from Skandia on 0345 697 186.

Contacts

Fund Manager
Simon Baker. 0171 314 4768

Jupiter Environmental Research Unit
Emma Howard Boyd 0171 314 4769
Charles Millar 0171 314 4770
Michael Tyrrell 0171 314 4772

Fax 0171 581 3857

Jupiter Asset Management
Knightsbridge House
197 Knightsbridge
London
SW7 1RB

Tel 0171 412 0703
Fax 0171 581 3857

FURTHER READING

Elkington, J and Burke, T (1987) *Green Capitalists,* Gollancz Ltd., London

Schmidheimy, S and Zorraquin, F (1996) *Financing Change: The Financial Community, Eco-Efficiency, and Sustainable Development*, MIT Press, Cambridge, Massachusetts

Spencer-Cooke, A (1994) *Where Silence is Not Golden: Towards the Strategic Use of Corporate Environmental Information for Company Valuation*, Association of Chartered Certified Accountants, occasional report, London

BIBLIOGRAPHY

Advisory Committee on Business and the Environment (1997) *Seventh Progress Report to and Response from the President of the Board of Trade and the Secretary of State for the Environment*, Department of the Environment/Department of Trade and Industry, London

Arthur D Little (1995) *The Environmental Performance Index*, Perspectives Series, Arthur D Little, Cambridge

Belkaoiu, A (1976) *The Impact of the Disclosure of the Environmental Effects of Organisational Behaviour on the Market*, Financial Management, Winter pp 26–30

BSI (1994) *Specification for Environmental Management Systems*, British Standards Institution, London

Cairncross, F (1991) *Costing the Earth*, Harvard Business School Press, Boston, Massachusetts

Cairncross, F (1994) *The Challenge of Going Green*, Harvard Business Review, Jul–Aug 1994, pp 40–41

Campanale et al (1993) *Survey of Ethical and Environmental Funds in Continental Europe*, Jupiter Tyndall Merlin, London

CBI (1994) *Environment Costs: The Effects on Competitiveness of Environment Health and Safety*, CBI, London

Chitty, G (1988) *Green Investors*, Green Pages, pp 188–189, Routledge, London

Clough, R (1997) *Environmental Screens and Portfolio Performance: A Comparative Analysis*, Winslow Environmental News, US

Company Reporting (1994) *Environmental Information*, No. 27, Sept 1992, Edinburgh

Cohen, M, Fenn, S and Naimon, J (1995) *Environmental and Financial Performance: Are They Related?*, IRRC Paper, Environmental Information Service, Washington DC

Cook, L (23 May 1992) '*Clear conscience, clear profit*', The Times, London

Cuthbert, J (12 Feb 1994) '*Performance, the Only Way to Judge a Trust's Worth*', The Financial Times, London

Cuthbert, J (15 June 1994) '*Assessing International Risks*', The Financial Times, London

Daly, H (1990) *Toward a Steady State Economy*, Louisiana State University, US

Department of the Environment (1997) *The Wider Costs and Benefits of Environmental Policy: A Discussion Paper*, DoE, London

Eaglesham, J (24 March 1996) 'Green funds reap moral rewards', *Independent on Sunday*, London

EIRIS (1988) *The Financial Performance of Ethical Investments*, 4.01 Bondsway Business Centre, London

Elkington, J and Burke, T (1987) *Green Capitalists*, Gollancz Ltd, London

Environmental Protection Agency (1990) *Environmental Investments: The Cost of a Clean Environment*, U.S. Government Printing Office, Washington DC

Erfle, S and Fratantuono, M (1992) *Interrelations Among Corporate Social Performance, Social Disclosure and Financial Performance: An Empirical Investigation*, Working paper, Dickinson College, US

Feldman, S, Soyka, P and Ameer P (1997) *Does Improving a Firm's Environmental Management System and Environmental Performance Result in a Higher Stock Price?*, ICF Kaiser International Inc, Fairfax, Virginia

Fischer, K and Schot, J (1994) *The Challenge of Going Green*, Harvard Business Review, Jul–Aug 1994, pp 47–48

Ghemawat, P (1986) *Sustainable Advantage*, Sept–Oct 1986, Harvard Business Review, Boston, Massachusetts

Gray, R (1994) *The Challenge of Going Green*, Harvard Business Review, Jul–Aug 1994, pp 46–47, Boston, Massachusetts

Greenwood, B (Oct 1995) *Environmental Law: Recent Developments and Practical Effects*, Norton Rose Environmental Law Group, London

Hamilton, J (1995) *Pollution as News: Media and Stock Market Reactions to Toxic Release Inventory Data*, Journal of Environmental Economics and Management, vol.28, pp 98–113

Hart, S and Ahuja, G (1994) *Does it Pay to be Green? – An Empirical Examination of the Relationship Between Pollution Prevention and Firm Performance*, University of Michigan, School of Business Administration, Michigan, US

Hillary, R (1995) *Small Firms and the Environment*, A Groundwork Status Report with Imperial College Centre of Environmental Technology, London

Holden Meehan (1996) *Independent Guide to Ethical and Green Investment Funds*, 6th Edition, Holden Meehan, London

Howarth, D (1989) *Environmental Investment : Opportunities in UK Unit Trusts*, MSc degree thesis, Imperial College of Science and Technology, London

Ilinitch, A and Schaltegger, S (April 1995) *Developing a Green Business Portfolio*, Long Range Planning, Vol. 28, No.2, pp 29–38

Investors Chronicle (10 Dec 1993) '*Rewards in heaven and on earth: Investing ethically does not have to hit your pocket*', London

Investors Chronicle (17 Sept 1993) '*Finding Tomorrow's Growth Stocks*', London

James Capel (1989) *The James Capel Green Book*, Steer, T and Hardman, R, James Capel, 6 Bevis Marks, London

Jupiter Environmental Research Unit (1995) *The Assessment Process for Green Investment Third Edition*, Jupiter Asset Management Limited, London

Jupiter Environmental Research Unit (1995) *Packaging Survey*, Jupiter Asset Management Limited, London, Unpublished document

Jupiter Environmental Research Unit (1996) *Report on the General Retail Sector Survey*, Jupiter Asset Management Limited, London, Unpublished document

Jupiter Environmental Research Unit (1997) *The Assessment Process for Green Investment Fourth Edition*, Jupiter Asset Management Limited, London

Kleiner A (1991) *What Does it Mean to be Green?*, Harvard Business Review 69, pp 38–47

Knight, P (1 Feb 1995) '*More May Be Less: Companies Claim that Published Green Expenditure is Increasingly Misleading*', The Financial Times, London

Knight P (1 Nov 1995) '*Attention Seekers in the Financial Market: Campaign groups are putting institutional investors under pressure to take action*', The Financial Times, London

KPMG (1995) *The Eco-Management and Audit Scheme: An Introductory Guide*, KPMG, London

Mahapatra, S (1984) *Investor Reaction to Corporate Social Accounting*, Journal of Business Finance and Accounting, Vol.11, pp 29–40

Marcus, A, Bromiley, P, and Goodman, R (1987) *Preventing Corporate Crises: Stock Market Losses as a Deterrent to the Production of Hazardous Products*, Columbia Journal of World Business, Spring, pp 33–42

McLean, R and Shopley, J (Aug 1996) '*Green Light Shows for Corporate Gains*', The Financial Times, London

O'Connor, A (1994) *Wiring up the Future: An Environmental Survey of the Electronics Industry*, Merlin Research Unit, Jupiter Tyndall Merlin, London

Pearson, P and Fouquet, R (1996) *Notes on the Relationship Between Care for the Environment and Market Gain*, Imperial College Centre for Environmental Technology, London

Piesse, J (Spring 1992) *Environmental Spending and Share Price Performance: The Petroleum Industry*, Business Strategy and the Environment, Vol. 1, Part 1, pp 45–52

Poole and Mansley (1996) *Nottinghamshire County Council Superannuation Fund Long Term Investment Strategy – Company Analysis*, Public and Corporate Economic Consultants Unpublished document

Porter, M (1991) *America's Green Strategy*, Scientific American, April 1991, p 168, New York

Porter, M and van der Linde, C (1995) *Green and Competitive: Ending the Stalemate*, Harvard Business Review, Sept–Oct 1995, pp 120–134

Rooney, C (Summer 1993) *Economics of Pollution Prevention: How Waste Reduction Pays*, Pollution Prevention Review, New York

Rubenstein D (1994) *Environmental Accounting for the Sustainable Corporation*, Quorum Books, Westport, Connecticut

Ryall, C and Ruby, S (1994) *Green Investment: An Incentive for Business*, Greener Management International, 1/1994, pp 16–21

Schmidheimy et al (1992) *Changing Course*, MIT Press, Cambridge, Massachusetts

Schmidheimy, S and Zorraquin, F (1995) *Financing Change: The Financial Community, Eco-Efficiency, and Sustainable Development*, MIT Press, Cambridge, Massachusetts

Schmalensee, R (1993) *The Costs of Environmental Protection*, Center for Energy and Environmental Policy Research, MIT, Cambridge, Massachusetts

Schoenberger, N (1993) *Green Funds: An Instrument of Change. A Study of Green Funds, Shareholder Power and Corporate Response*, Wye College, London

Shephard F (Sept 1995) *Does Care for the Environment Yield Market Gain?*, International Gas Union Mini Conference, Prague

Shrivastava, P and Hart, A (1992) *Greening Organisations*, Academy of Management Best Paper Proceedings, vol. 52, pp 185–189, US

Slater J (July 1997), *Company REFS: Really Essential Financial Statistics*, Hemmington Scott Publishing Limited, London

Smart, B (1994) *The Challenge of Going Green*, Harvard Business Review, Jul–Aug 1994, pp 42–43

Spencer-Cooke, A (1994) *Where Silence is Not Golden: Towards the Strategic Use of Corporate Environmental Information for Company Valuation*, ACCA Occasional Research Paper, London

Stavins R, Jaffe A, Peterson S, Portney P (1994) *The Challenge of Going Green*, Harvard Business Review, Jul–Aug 1994, pp 38–39

UNEP (Sept 1994) *Environmental Credit Risk Management*, UNEP Meeting on Banks and the Environment, Sept 26–27, UNEP Offices, Geneva

US EPA (1995) *An Introduction to Environmental Accounting as a Business Tool*, Reprinted by ACCA

Walley, N and Whitehead B (1994) *The Challenge of Going Green*, Harvard Business Review, Jul–Aug 1994, pp 48–49

Wells, R (1994) *The Challenge of Going Green*, Harvard Business Review, Jul–Aug 1994, pp 43–44

Wyld A (1993) *The Role and Future of British Green and Ethical Funds*, Imperial College Centre for Environmental Technology, London

INDEX

For Product Safety Concerns and Information please contact our EU
representative GPSR@taylorandfrancis.com Taylor & Francis Verlag GmbH,
Kaufingerstraße 24, 80331 München, Germany

Printed and bound by CPI Group (UK) Ltd, Croydon, CR0 4YY

08/05/2025

01864544-0001